Overheard at the Country Cafe

**A collection
of more than 500
good clean jokes
you can tell your
preacher, priest or rabbi.**

Acknowledgments

Tom Keegan of Wamego, Kansas supplied many of the jokes that appear in this volume. Tom is an avid reader of Reiman Publications magazines and books, who frequently shares clever quips with his fellow readers across the country.

Thanks, too, are due Msgr. Arthur Tonne for permission to reprint some of the jokes that appear in his books. He's the prolific author of *Jokes Priests Can Tell*, a nine-volume set (soon to be 10!). For more information on his books, write Msgr. Tonne at 520 N. Freeborn, Marion, Kansas 66861.

Finally, thanks to Ken Alley for jokes from his collection *Once Upon a Pew*. For more information about this book, write Ken at P.O. Box 552, York, Nebraska 68467.

Contents

Editor: Mike Beno
Assistant Editors: Deb Mulvey,
Jean Steiner, Jerry Wiebel
Art Director: Linda Dzik
Production: Ellen Lloyd, Claudia Wardius
Photo Coordinator: Anne Schimmel
Cartoon Coordinator: Mary Ann Koebernik
Publisher: Roy J. Reiman

On the Cover: Now *that's* a good one!
These folks share a friendly joke at Ted's
Ice Cream & Restaurant, Wauwatosa, Wisconsin.
Photo by Scott Anderson.

Country Books
International Standard Book Number: 0-89821-238-3
Library of Congress Catalog Card Number: 98-67163

For additional copies of this book or information
on other books, write: Country Books, P.O. Box
990, Greendale WI 53129. Credit card orders call
toll-free: 1-800/558-1013.

Introduction

WHERE CAN YOU FIND good clean humor these days? Reiman Publications magazines, of course! Thanks to our readers, they're *filled* with fun.

Because our readers basically "write" all 10 of our magazines, we rely on them to supply the chuckles we print on our humor pages. And do these folks ever come through!

Not only do our subscribers seem to have an inexhaustible supply of jokes, they liberally share the smiles with fellow readers all across the country.

Subscribers to *Country* magazine, for example, have laughed together for years over jokes in our popular column, "Overheard at the Country Cafe". This department is *always* filled with good clean fun!

Smiles Across the Miles

Likewise, *Reminisce* readers share smiles across the miles through that magazine's humor pages, titled "Over the Backfence". This feature is another reader favorite.

And *Country Woman* subscribers are perennially pleased to share the most clever quips from the lips of children in that magazine's long-running feature, "From the Mouths of Little Sprouts".

Because these pages are so popular, we finally decided to give in to our readers' requests that we publish a book of clean humor...jokes you could tell your preacher, priest or rabbi.

When we asked the readers of those magazines to send their favorite jokes, cracks and quips for this book, we were *buried* in belly laughs. So much so, that we've packed more than 500 jokes (plus quips and cartoons) into this hardcover volume of humor.

So, why not settle back in a comfy chair and get ready to enjoy a hearty chuckle or two? Thanks to our readers, we're sure you'll find more than a few!

Chapter One

Farmers and City Slickers

Whether from town
or country, you're
likely to locate
some laughs in
this chapter.

"No, you can *not* run your manure spreader through here!"

Where Are We?

A FARMER and his wife were having a friendly argument about whether a town in Pennsylvania was pronounced LAN-caster or LANC-aster. The farmer decided to drive there and find out how the natives pronounced it.

He stopped at the first business place in town, took his wife by the hand and walked in. He said to the clerk, "Now tell my wife the name of this place, and speak very slowly and distinctly." The clerk looked at them for a moment, then enunciated slowly, and very carefully, "Bur-ger King".

—*Leanna Adler Rudolph, Ohio*

Sparked an Idea

A FARMER had never been to a big-city restaurant before, and the maitre d' wouldn't admit him without a necktie. "Don't you have one you could loan me?" the farmer asked.

"They're all loaned out," the maitre d' replied.

Undaunted, the farmer returned to his pickup, hoping to find something he could use as a necktie. Soon he was back inside with a pair of jumper cables tied around his neck.

"Will this do?" he asked. "Well, okay," the maitre d' said. "But don't start anything." —*Sid Allsbury*
Springfield, Missouri

An Open Letter...

TO THE Honorable Secretary of Agriculture:

My friend, LaVerne Swenson, got a check from you for $1,000 for not raising hogs. So, I want to go into the "not raising hogs" business next year.

What I want to know is, what is the best kind of farm not to raise hogs on? And what is the best breed of hogs not to raise? As I see it, the hardest part of not raising hogs is keeping records on how many hogs I haven't raised.

My friend Swenson is very happy about the future of the hog business. He raised hogs for 20 years, and the most he ever made in one year was $422.90. However, this year he got your check for $1,000 for not raising 50 hogs.

If I get $1,000 for not raising 50 hogs, would I get $2,000 for not raising 100 hogs? I plan to start on a small scale, but hope to work up to not raising 4,000 hogs, which would bring in about $80,000.

Now, one more thing. Those hogs I won't raise will not eat 100,000 bushels of corn. I understand the government also pays people not to raise corn and wheat. I want to know if I would qualify for payments for not raising those crops.

I'm also giving serious thought to not milking cows, and any details you can give me on that program will be appreciated. Since I will be totally unemployed, I will be filing for unemployment and food stamps, and would appreciate it if you would send the forms along with the information I've asked about.

Patriotically yours, Ole

P.S. Maybe you can tell me when you plan to give out free cheese again?
  —*Norman Nelson*
Wilson, Wisconsin

Don't Let the Bedbugs...Snap?

SOME CATTLEMEN were showing a Texas rancher around Kansas City. "What do you think of the stockyards?" they asked.

"Oh, they're all right," the visitor said. "But in Texas, we have branding corrals that are bigger."

That night, the men put some turtles in the Texan's bed. When he turned back the covers and saw them, he asked what they were.

"Missouri bedbugs," the men replied.

"So they are," the Texan agreed. "Young 'uns, aren't they?"

Don't Get Caught In the Rain

AN OLD FARMER was visiting a neighbor when a downpour started. It looked as if the rain would continue for hours.

"You'd better spend the night here," the neighbor suggested. The farmer looked out at the heavy rain and agreed.

The neighbor left the room for a few minutes to put on a pot of coffee. When he came back, the old farmer was standing in the living room, soaking wet.

"What happened?" the neighbor asked.

The farmer replied, "I had to run home and get my pajamas."

—*Mrs. Edward Kisabeth*
Fostoria, Ohio

Dairy Discouraging

A MILK TRUCK stopped at a dairy farm on its regular rounds. A herd of cows stood in a nearby pasture, idly grazing.

The truck had a sign on it reading, "Our Milk is Pasteurized, Homogenized and Fortified with Vitamins A and D."

One cow looked at the sign and said to another, "Makes you feel downright inadequate, doesn't it?"

It's a Long Way Up

OLE WAS STANDING next to a flagpole while a friend stood on his shoulders, holding a tape measure. A man walked by and asked, "What are you doing?"

"Measuring the flagpole," Ole said.

"It would be easier to find the length with the pole lying down," the observer said.

"We already know the length," Ole said. "We want to find out the height."

—Marvin Schuck
Brewster, Minnesota

Who's Foolin' Who?

A FELLOW from the big city was driving through a rural area when he saw a boy standing alongside the road with a sign that read "Puppy for Sale". The man thought the little urchin was cute, so he stopped and paid him $10 for the dog.

As the man prepared to drive away, he called to the boy, "Be careful with that money, son. Remember the saying, 'A fool and his money are soon parted'."

"Yep," the tike said. "But I want to thank you for parting with it just the same."

Must Be Where Race Horses Come From

A CITY SLICKER heard that a farm was a good place to live, so he bought one. After moving in, he saw a farmer across the fence, plowing with horses. The city slicker walked over and asked how he could get some horses.

"You have to hatch them," the farmer said. "I have a couple extra eggs you can have." Then he handed the city slicker two large pumpkins.

On the way home, the city slicker dropped one of the pumpkins. It rolled into a rock and burst open. From behind that rock, a frightened rabbit took off like a shot.

The city slicker gave chase, but the rabbit just got farther and farther away. "To heck with you," he yelled after it. "You're too fast for the plow anyway."

—Ralph Berg
Brooks, Minnesota

"Mow your lawn, mister?"

What's the Special?

A CITY SLICKER went into a restaurant for dinner. The waiter said, "May I recommend the special today, sir? It's calf's tongue."

"Calf's tongue!" the city slicker retorted. "Do you expect me to eat something that's been in an animal's mouth?"

He studied the menu for a minute, then ordered an omelet. —*Harry Kenyon Mitchell, Nebraska*

Them's the Breaks

WATCHING her father working on his tractor, the little farm girl asked her mother, "What happens to old tractors when they finally stop working?"

Sighing, her mother answered, "Someone sells them to your father, dear."

Oh, Never Mind

A SMALL BARN burned down on an older couple's farm. The couple had insured it for $50,000, so the farmer's wife called their insurance agent and asked him to send a check.

"It doesn't work that way," the agent replied. "We'll come and replace the barn."

"Oh," the farmer's wife said. "Well, if that's how you do business, I'd better cancel the insurance on my husband." —*Philip Hershey Ashland, Ohio*

Now *That's* a Dry Spell

"HOW'S the drought out your way?" a Kansas farmer asked his friend.

"Pretty bad," the other farmer replied. "Just yesterday, two of my cows started giving powdered milk."

This One's a Howler!

A FARMER took his dog to a small-town movie theater and sat the pooch beside him in a seat.

The dog watched the film attentively, howling with laughter at the funny scenes.

After the show, another theater patron who'd been seated nearby stopped the farmer in the lobby. "It's really amazing how your dog enjoyed the movie," he said.

"It sure is," the farmer agreed. "He hated the book!"

Bull Market

A MAN DRIVING a pickup truck pulled alongside the barn and hailed the farmer. "How much is that old bull out by the road worth?" the visitor asked.

"Well, that depends," the farmer said slowly. "Are you the tax assessor, do you want to buy him or did you run him down with your truck?"

The Man Loves His Work

A CITY MAN visiting a dairy farmer asked, "Do you really like milking all these cows?"

"I don't mind it," the farmer replied. "Sometimes I even get a kick out of it."

Case Closed

A FARMER walked into an attorney's office to see about a divorce.

"Do you have grounds?" the attorney asked.

"Yeah, I got about 140 acres," the farmer replied.

"No, you don't understand," the attorney said.

"Do you have a case?"

The farmer said, "No, I don't have a Case, but I have an old John Deere."

"No, no. I mean, do you have a grudge?"

"Yeah, I got a grudge," the farmer replied. "That's where I park my John Deere."

In desperation, the attorney asked, "Does your wife beat you up or anything?"

The farmer replied, "No, sir. We both get up about 4:30. But she gets mighty cranky by supper time, and that's why I want a divorce."

—*Roger Hagemann*
Wells, Minnesota

But Who Gets To Drive?

OLE AND LENA were having a serious talk. "Ole, we both know how sick I am," Lena said. "Before long I'll be gone to my reward. There's just one thing I want you to promise me. I want you and my mother to ride in the same car in the funeral procession."

After a bit, Ole said, "Well, okay. But you know it will ruin my whole day."

—*Roger Westerberg*
Verndale, Minnesota

Don't Count Your Chickens

OLE WAS A FARMER in the old country. One day he decided to try raising chickens and ordered 300 "starter chicks" from the co-op. About a week later, he returned and said every single chick had died.

The clerk was dumbfounded. He contacted the hatchery, which sent out 300 new starter chicks, plus an extra 50 to make up for the farmer's inconvenience.

Ole took them home, but a week later he was back again. The clerk was flabbergasted and called the hatchery again. This time they sent Ole 400 chicks.

Alas, a week later he was back with the same complaint. The clerk called the hatchery and asked what to do. They suggested Ole send one of the chicks to the Ministry of Agriculture and ask for an opinion, which he did.

"I am enclosing one of my dead starter chicks," Ole wrote. "Am I planting them too deep, or is there another problem?"

"I don't know," the Minister of Agriculture wrote back. "Send us a soil sample."

—Don Meyer, Elma, Iowa

"Good news and bad.
We've struck oil...but it's corn oil."

I'm Here to Help You...

A GOVERNMENT MAN came to see what a farmer was paying his help. There was a hired man, a hired girl and an idiot who worked for room and board.

The farmer said the hired man got to use the pickup truck twice a week in addition to his wages. The government man said that seemed all right. The hired girl watched soap operas half the time, so her wages seemed all right, too.

Then the government man said, "Now I want to talk to the idiot who just works for room and board."

The farmer said, "You're talking to him."

—David Bowman
Pierceton, Indiana

This Little Piggy

A 5-YEAR-OLD, visiting a farm for the first time, was looking at a fat sow lying in a pen.

"She's mighty big, isn't she?" said the farmer.

"She should be," said the youngster. "I just saw six little piggies blowing her up a few minutes ago."

Let's See Some ID

A STRANGER approached a farmer, showed him an identification card and announced, "I'm a government inspector and am entitled to inspect your farm."

A while later, the farmer heard a scream from the alfalfa patch. On investigating, he found the inspector was being chased by a bull. The farmer leaned over the gate and yelled, "Show him your card, mister!"

Dream On

THE DEAN of the agriculture school was interviewing a freshman. "Why have you chosen this career?" he asked.

"I dream of making a million dollars in farming like my father did," the student said.

The dean was impressed. "Your father made a million dollars in farming?"

"No," the student said, "but he's always dreamed of it."

Digging a Hole...or Two

A FARMER'S cow died, so he pulled it out to the field and began digging a hole. Soon his neighbor noticed he was digging a second hole and then a third. The neighbor walked over and asked, "Why are you digging three holes to bury one cow?"

The farmer looked up and explained, "The first two weren't deep enough."

Picture This

AT A RURAL ART exhibit, a farmer walked up to an abstract painting and looked at it from all angles. Finally he told his wife he wanted to buy it.

When she asked why, he said, "It's the best darned picture of the farm situation I've ever seen. No matter which way you look at it, it doesn't make sense."

"Time these farmers out West learned about contour plowing."

The Hero's a Ham

A TRAVELING SALESMAN was passing a farm when he saw a pig with a wooden leg. Curiosity got the best of him, and he stopped to ask about it.

"One night our house caught fire, and that pig dug under the fence and crashed through the window," the farmer explained. "He woke us all up and saved us. He sure is a special pig!

"And one day my tractor tipped over and trapped me underneath. That pig came out, dug the dirt out from around me and saved my life. Yep, that sure is a special pig."

The salesman scratched his head and said, "That's all well and good, but why does he have a wooden leg?"

"Shucks," the farmer said, "you wouldn't want to eat a special pig like that all at once."   —Don Meyer
Elma, Iowa

Truck Farming

A TEXAS RANCHER, bragging about the size of his place, told an Iowa farmer, "My ranch is so big I can drive my pickup all day and not get to the edge of it."

"Yep," replied the Iowa farmer. "I had a pickup like that once."

He's Well Cultivated

First Farmer: "How's that new neighbor of yours doing, the one with the college degree?"

Second Farmer: Oh, all right, I guess. He's just a little different. See, he farms strictly with horses. And when he reaches the end of the field, instead of saying, 'Whoa, haw and gee', he says, 'Halt, Rebecca, pivot and proceed'."

A Bolt from The Blue

MANY YEARS AGO, the telephone company wanted to extend a line from the city to the country. One old farmer doubted it was possible to talk through a wire, but agreed to pay his share of the expense if it worked.

When the line was completed, a telephone company representative ran into the farmer in town. "Come on up to the office," the phone man said. "You can talk to your wife out on the farm."

A fierce thunderstorm came up after they entered the building. Lightning struck the wire just as the farmer's wife said, "Is that you, John?"

The electric shock knocked him to the floor. The farmer got up and said with a grin, "That's Mary, all right. I'll pay my share."

How Many Bushels To the Acre?

DID YOU HEAR Illinois corn farmers have a bumper crop this year? It's usually up to the windshield. This year it's up to the bumper.
          —Jason Craig
DeKalb County, Illinois

Let's Make It Legal

A CITY FELLOW moved to the country. He depended on advice from books and pamphlets and a friendly neighboring farmer to help him learn.

One day he decided to kill his first chicken, so he rounded up the intended victim and tucked the bird under his arm, along with a book about poultry processing.

Back behind the barn, with the chicken still under his arm, he opened the book and began reading. Suddenly, he looked up and saw his farmer friend taking in the scene.

"What are you doing?" the farmer inquired. "Reading him his rights?"

Stupid is As Stupid Does

ON RAINY DAYS, the farmers in our town liked to hang out at the feed mill. But the mill owner would use this time to berate his employees for their stupidity.

One wet day when the mill was full of farmers, the boss started ridiculing one of his workers. "You're the stupidest dunce whoever worked here," he said. "You are dumb, dumb, dumb."

The employee replied, "I guess you're right, boss. I worked here 3 years before I found out there was more than 1,700 lbs. in a ton."

—*Earl Chapman*
Springfield, Ohio

Won't You Join Me?

AN OLD FARMER rounded a curve on a country road and crashed into an oncoming car driven by a city-slicker salesman.

As the men sat at the edge of the road waiting for the police, the old farmer turned to the salesman and said, "You look a little shook. I have a bottle of whiskey in my truck. Want a drink?"

The salesman said that might help his nerves. He took a long pull on the bottle, handed it back and said, "Well, old-timer, are you going to have a drink, too?"

"Yep," the farmer said as he put the cap back on the bottle. "But I think I'll have mine after the sheriff leaves."   —*Greg Smoker*
Wanatah, Indiana

Take a Look Around

THE CITY SLICKER asked his cousin, "What time do you go to work?"

"I don't go to work," the farmer answered. "I wake up with work all around me."

One Coat or Two?

A FARMER hired a fellow to paint his barn. At the end of the first day, the farmer found the worker had painted only 60 boards on one side of the barn.

The second day he painted 40 boards, and the third day, only 20. "What is this?" complained the farmer. "Every day you paint less and less."

"It's not my fault!" the worker snapped back. "Each day I get farther and farther from the paint can!"

"Speaking of creamed carrots, did your son tell you what he did to the tractor?"

I'm Fine, Thanks

A FARMER was driving his prize cow to a cattle sale when a semi truck swerved into his lane and slammed into his pickup. When the farmer came to, his truck was overturned, and the cow lay bruised and bleeding in the ditch.

A state trooper arrived, saw the cow was suffering and shot her twice. Then he peered into the pickup and asked the farmer how he felt.

The farmer looked up and said, in a quavering voice, "I've never felt better in my life."

High-Octane Fuel

A VETERINARIAN was motoring along when he came upon a farmer having problems with a balky mule.

"Can you give him anything that'll make him go?" asked the farmer.

The vet opened his bag, took out some powders and gave them to the mule. After a moment the mule galloped off down the road in an astonishing burst of speed.

"How much will that dose be?" asked the farmer.

"Oh, $5, I guess," said the vet.

"Then give me a $10 dose quick," demanded the farmer. "I gotta catch that mule!"

Now, See Here

A FELLOW from New York City was driving along the coast of Maine and stopped to ask a native how to find the covered bridge in Littleton.

"Well," the man drawled, "you just go three C's and then head north."

"What are three C's?" the city man asked.

"You just head down the road for as far as you can see, and then do it again twice."

They're Circling

AN OLD MAN was sitting on the porch of his small-town store when a big shiny car drove up with two strangers in it. "Hey, Grandpa," one of them called to the man, "how long has this burg been dead?"

The old man looked over his spectacles and slowly replied, "Not long, I reckon.

You're the first buzzards I've seen."

Giving It All She's Got

PRESIDENT Dwight Eisenhower used to tell this story about his father's attempt to buy a cow from a neighbor.

Mr. Eisenhower started out by asking the old farmer about the cow's pedigree. But the farmer didn't know what "pedigree" meant.

Then Mr. Eisenhower asked about the cow's butterfat production. The farmer said he didn't know anything about that.

Finally, Mr. Eisenhower asked the farmer if he knew how many pounds of milk the cow produced each year. The farmer shook his head and said, "I don't know, but she's an honest old cow, and she'll give you all the milk she has."

—*Ada Johnson*
Kalamazoo, Michigan

God Got It Right

A FARMER and his wife spent the morning loading their pumpkin crop onto a truck. When they finished, they sat in the shade of an oak tree to rest.

The farmer began musing about the nature of things and told his wife, "You know, God made a mistake. He put those big pumpkins on small vines and tiny acorns on this big oak tree. If I were God, I'd have put the small fruit on small plants and big fruit on big plants."

Just then a squirrel scampered through the tree overhead, sending a shower of acorns down on their heads. The farmer's wife turned to her husband and said, "Lucky for us you're not God."

You Can't Get There from Here

A SALESMAN lost in a maze of Pennsylvania back roads happened upon a farmer sitting on a fence.

"I don't do windrows."

The salesman pulled over and called, "Old-timer, how do I get to Flatville?"

"I can't say," the farmer drawled.

"Well, then, do you know the way to Wilson?"

"Nope."

"How about the way to Carterville?"

"Can't remember," the farmer said.

Exasperated, the salesman shouted, "You're not very smart, are you?"

"Maybe not," the farmer said. "But I ain't lost."

—G.R. Smith
Aurora, Colorado

Going Hog Wild

A FARMER was driving toward Jacksonville, Florida when he saw a pig wandering down the interstate.

Fearing someone would run it over, the farmer stopped and picked up the animal, then put it on the seat next to him.

A few minutes later, he was stopped by a highway patrolman. "I can appreciate your love for animals, but you should take that pig to the zoo," the patrolman said. "Okay," the farmer said, and he drove off.

A week later, the farmer was driving down the same road with the pig sitting next to him. The highway patrolman stopped him again. "I thought I told you to take that pig to the zoo," the patrolman said.

"I did," the farmer said. "And he had such a good time that today we're going to Disney World."

—Denny Brake
Raleigh, North Carolina

Hiring and Firing

A FARMER was looking over the work record of a farm hand seeking a job. "It looks to me as if you've been fired from every job you've ever held," the farmer said, shaking his head.

"Well," the hand grinned, "that proves I'm no quitter."

Godspeed

A TOURIST passing through a small town asked one of the residents, "What's the speed limit through this one-horse town of yours?"

"Ain't got one," the native replied. "You folks can't go through here fast enough to suit us."

Behind the Wheel

TWO FARMERS were chatting over coffee at the local diner. "I see your son is driving a car now," said one. "How long did it take him to learn?"

"About 2-1/2 cars," replied the other farmer sadly.

Face Looks Familiar

AN OLD FARMER was working in the field when he found a piece of mirror. He looked into it and said, "It's my dad!" He looked at the mirror again and again, and put it under his pillow at bedtime.

After he fell asleep, his curious wife reached under his pillow, pulled out the mirror and peered into it.

"Just as I thought," she said. "Another woman. And an ugly one, too."

—*Ardina Van Schyndel*
Elkhorn, Wisconsin

He Saw the Light

A FARMER and his wife were expecting. When the doctor came to deliver the baby, he said he needed more light, so the farmer got a lantern from the barn. The doctor told him to bring the light closer.

"Well," the doctor said after a while, "you have a fine baby boy." The farmer smiled. Then the doctor told him to bring the lantern close again. After a few more minutes, he announced another arrival— this time, a baby girl. The farmer began walking away with the lantern.

"Where are you going?" the doctor asked.

"I'm getting this light out of here," the farmer replied. "I think it's attracting them."

—*Vern Onhen*
Slayton, Minnesota

Plowing for Votes

THE POMPOUS politician was winding up what he considered a stirring, fact-filled campaign speech. As he finished, he looked out over the rural audience and asked, "Now, then...are there any questions?"

A farmer in bib overalls stood up and replied, "Only one. Who else is running?"

"It's not snowing in August.
This heat wave got to your popcorn."

Old Reliable

THE AGED FARMER was in bad shape, with no more than 24 hours to live. He told his wife he wanted to be buried with his John Deere tractor, with the chains on. Asked why, he explained, "I've never seen a hole yet that John Deere and chains couldn't get me out of."
—*Floyd Reif, Wapello, Iowa*

Jurisprudence

A JURY consists of 12 people who decide which side has the slicker lawyer.
—*John Edinborough Gooding, Idaho*

"Wow! When your dad digs for fishing worms, he doesn't fool around!"

He Knows, He Knows

DRIVING along a country road, a seed corn salesman spotted a farmer slowly cultivating his corn with an old mule.

The salesman stopped his car, leaned over the fence at the end of the field and tried to sell the farmer some seed corn for the next year.

"Your corn looks sorta yellow," the salesman told the farmer.

"I know," the farmer said, "I planted yellow corn."

"Well," the salesman persisted, "it looks like you only get half a crop."

"I know," the farmer said, "I only farm for half."

Exasperated, the salesman said, "Seems to me there isn't much separating you from a fool."

"I know," the farmer replied, "just this fence."

Never Sausage An Appetite

GRANDMA was planning a cookout for her 9-year-old grandson, who was visiting the farm.

"How many hot dogs can you eat?" she asked him.

The youngster shrugged. "I don't know—Mom always stops me before I can find out!"

Logic by the Bunch

A NEW BRIDE was proudly showing her first garden to a friend.

The friend noticed several green clusters at the end of the plot and asked what was growing there.

"Radishes," the bride beamed.

"That's interesting," the friend commented. "Most gardeners plant them in rows."

"They do?" puzzled the bride. "But they always come in bunches at the store."

A Bargain He Could Handle

A FARMER went to the hardware store and bought five hammer handles at $5 each. The next day, he came back and bought five more. The third day, he returned and asked for another five.

"I'm all out," the clerk said. "There's not much demand for hammer handles around here. What are you doing with all of them?"

"Oh, I'm reselling them for $3 each," the farmer said.

"Wait a minute," the clerk said. "You're buying them for $5 and reselling them for $3?"

"Yep," the farmer said. "It sure beats farming."

—Dutch Collins
Marengo, Ohio

Farm Mom: "I don't like all those pesky flies."
Farm Boy: "Okay—point out the ones you like, and I'll swat the rest."

That Ain't Chicken Scratch

"HOW MUCH are your chickens?" inquired a motorist stopped at a farmer's roadside market.

"Fifty cents a pound," replied the farmer.

"Did you raise them yourself?"

"Yep. They were 45¢ yesterday."

Deserves a Salute

A CITY COUPLE had just moved to a small rural area, and they asked a neighboring farmer for some advice.

What, they inquired, would be good to plant in a spot that gets very little rain, has too much late-afternoon sun, has clay soil and is on a rocky ledge?

"Well," replied the farmer thoughtfully, "how about a nice flagpole?"

Rural Daffynitions

Poor Wheat Crop: *Amber Waves of Pain*
Infertile Egg: *A Little White Lie*
Transient Farm Hand: *Brawn But Not Forgotten*
Flood Control: *A Ditch in Time*
Unprofitable Herd: *Feed 'Em and Weep*

Went Nose-to-Nose

TWO FARMERS, each on a tractor pulling an extra-wide implement, met head-on at a narrow bridge. There wasn't enough room to pass and no room to turn around.

One farmer, a hot-tempered sort, shouted, "I'm not budging. I never back up for idiots!"

The other farmer snorted and shifted into reverse. "That's okay!" he shouted back. "I always do!"

Sounds Like Bull-oney

A RETIREE wanted to make a few extra dollars, so he borrowed some money and bought cows. When the cows didn't calve, he talked to his banker. The banker said he needed a bull. So he sold the cows and bought a bull.   —*Hank Endress Wyoming, Illinois*

Doggone Funny

THE FARMER was watching a hunter who'd asked permission to hunt on his pond.

Each time the hunter bagged a duck, his dog would retrieve it by running out across the *top* of the water, then coming back completely *dry*.

After this had happened

several times, the hunter proudly asked the farmer, "Notice anything unusual about my dog?"

"Sure do," replied the farmer. "He can't swim."

noticed a fly in the milk bucket. "That's really something," he said. "A fly goes in one ear and out the udder." —*Vernon Schmucker Quincy, Michigan*

Headed Downstream

A FARMER was milking when he saw a fly disappear into the cow's ear. After milking a while longer, he

Doing Double Duty

"THIS MACHINE will do half your chores for you," the salesman told the farmer.

"In that case," the farmer drawled, "I'll take two."

"We've won a grant to research why lightning bugs don't get hit by lightning…"

The Tall and Short of It

THREE FARMERS were having coffee in the local cafe and reminiscing about seasons past.

"I never saw a worse summer than the one we had back in '49," said the first farmer. "My corn never grew taller than 1 inch!"

The second farmer nodded. "An inch? You had a *good* crop compared to mine—that summer the sparrows had to *kneel* to reach my corn!"

"I've got you both beat," insisted the third farmer. "My corn was so short that summer, I had to lather the field to cut it!"

Ears of Scorn

A FARM WIFE secretly arranged for her daughter to take voice lessons. One day, while the lass was vocaliz-

"These horse plowing contests sure have changed."

ing, her father came in unexpectedly from the fields.

"What's that funny noise?" the farmer asked.

"That," his wife replied, "is Mabel cultivating her voice."

"Cultivating?" the farmer snorted. "That's not cultivating, that's *harrowing*!"

Ears How the Z-Z-Z Ended Up In 'Lazy'

FEARING he was a bad example to their children, the pioneers of an 1800's Midwest community decided to "resettle" the laziest man in town elsewhere.

They loaded the unprotesting chap on a wagon. But as they approached the town limits, they met a kind-hearted farmer, who asked what was going on.

"This is the laziest man in the world," someone shouted, "and we're ashamed to have him around anymore."

"Come, come—no one can be *that* lazy," the farmer responded. "I'm sure he's just down on his luck. Here...I'll put up 5 bushels of corn to help this poor soul back on his feet."

Hearing the offer, the accused man tipped back his hat and asked suspiciously, "Is it shucked?"

How's That Again?

AFTER YEARS of driving tractors with blown-out mufflers, an old farmer told his neighbor he'd finally gotten a hearing aid. "What kind is it?" the neighbor asked.

"Two-thirty," the farmer replied. —*Richard Penland Auburn, Indiana*

Keepin' Tabs on Courtin'

OLD ZEKE was the biggest skinflint in the county, and he was worried about his son, who was courting a neighbor lass.

"I hope you're not spendin' any money on such foolishness," Zeke prodded one morning.

"Don't worry, Paw," the boy replied. "We only spent a dollar last night."

"A dollar!" Zeke exploded.

The boy shrugged. "Well, that was all she had."

Pigs Can't Climb Trees

A SEASONED farmer was headed to town for supplies when he spotted his new neighbor. The former city fellow was standing beneath an apple tree, holding a pig on his shoulders. The pig was happily munching on apples, and several other pigs were milling about, obviously waiting their turns.

The farmer called out, "Say, don't you think feeding your pigs that way is an awful waste of time?"

The novice strained to get the pig a little higher into the tree. "Nah," he replied. "Pigs don't have anything better to do with their time!"

Polly Want a New Owner?

A FARMER wandered into a fast-moving auction to pass the time. Before he knew it, he found he'd bought a parrot.

Disgusted with himself for being such a sucker, the man paid for the bird and started carrying it home. On the way, he ran into a friend and told him what he'd done. "I spent all that money," he complained, "and I'll bet this bird doesn't even talk."

The parrot glared at him and retorted, "Who do you think was bidding against you?"

Can You Top This?

TWO FARMERS were always trying to outdo each other. One morning the first farmer told his son, "Go over to Mr. Smith's house and borrow a crosscut saw. Tell him I want to cut a pumpkin."

The son came back and said, "Mr. Smith says you can't have the saw until this afternoon. He's halfway through a potato."

Easy Come, Easy Go

A LUCKY FARMER won $5 million in the lottery. "What are you going to do now?" a city friend asked. The farmer replied, "Just keep farming until it's gone."

—*Jill Williams*
Benton Harbor, Michigan

Strong Farm Hands Versus the Little Squirt

DURING their lunch break, a pair of young men on a citrus-picking crew got to

"I'm afraid you have pulled a hamstring."

boasting over who had the strongest grip. They decided to settle the matter by seeing who could squeeze the most juice from a lemon.

The first fellow filled half a Thermos cup with a single mighty squeeze. Then the second fellow filled his cup three-quarters full.

Just then, a car pulled up and a skinny fellow in a business suit got out to ask directions. When he saw what was going on, he asked if he could join the "squeeze-off". The burly farm boys laughingly agreed.

The little fellow plucked a lemon, gave it a squeeze... and filled a cup to overflowing!

"What do you do for a living, mister?" asked the astonished farm boys as the city slicker climbed back into his car.

The little guy smiled. "I'm with the IRS."

Chapter Two

Ask an Expert

They seem
to know it all...
which makes
them even more
funny when
they don't.
Leap in and laugh!

An Expert Opinion

"YOUR METHODS are a century behind the times," the pompous government expert told the lifelong farmer. "I'd be surprised if you got a bushel of wheat to the acre out of that field."

"So would I," the farmer agreed. "That's barley."

Sounds Reasonable

A MOTHER was trying to coax her son to get up and go to school. "Give me two reasons why you shouldn't go," she demanded.

"Well," he said, "all the teachers hate me and all the students hate me. Give me two reasons why I should go."

His mother replied firmly, "Because you're 42 years old, and you're the principal."
—*Tom Keegan*
Wamego, Kansas

Any Suggestions?

AT A POLITICAL BANQUET, several long-winded speakers covered nearly every subject imaginable.

When yet another speaker rose, he said, "It seems to me that everything has already been talked about. If someone will tell me what to talk about, I would be grateful."

A weary voice from the back of the room suggested, "Talk about a minute!"

I'm Only Here To Help

THREE PEOPLE were waiting in line at the Pearly Gates. The first told St. Peter he'd been a doctor for over 50 years and couldn't even count all the people he'd helped. St. Peter invited him in.

The next in line was a woman who'd been a nurse for 40 years. St. Peter told her she'd earned a place in Heaven, too.

Then St. Peter turned to the third person and asked what he'd done with his life. "I worked for Medicare for years," the man said. "Then I was the head of one of the biggest HMOs in the country. You can imagine how many people I've helped."

"Well, come on in," St. Peter sighed. "But you can only stay 2 days."
—*Mary Cunnyngham*
Cleveland, Tennessee

Chaotic Beginnings

A SURGEON, an engineer and a politician were arguing about whose profession was the oldest.

"Mine is," the doctor insisted. "Remember that Eve was carved out of Adam's rib."

"Maybe," said the engineer. "But the earth was created out of chaos in 6 days. That was obviously an engineering job."

"Yes," the politician agreed. "But who created the chaos?"

Serious Business

A YOUNG SURGEON received a call from a colleague inviting him over for a poker foursome.

"Called out, dear?" his wife asked sympathetically.

"I'm afraid so," the doctor replied bravely. "It's a serious case. There are three other doctors there already."

"Who needs to lay out a fortune for a plumber?"

Left Bad Taste In His Mouth

A LAWYER driving past a farmer's pasture stopped to watch a dog that was grabbing dried cow pies in its mouth, shaking them, then tossing them away.

After watching the dog do this several times, the lawyer said to the farmer, "That's an odd way for your dog to act, isn't it?"

"No," the farmer said. "You see, he bit a lawyer this morning, and he's trying to get the bad taste out of his mouth." —*Marilyn Seibert Spencerville, Ohio*

"I've read what distinguishes man from the lower species is the ability to use tools."

A Most Difficult Case

AN ILL-TEMPERED MAN went to see the doctor.

"What seems to be your trouble?" the doctor asked kindly.

"That's what you're supposed to tell me," the man retorted.

"In that case," the doctor said, "I'd like you to sit in the reception room for about an hour while I call a specialist. He's a veterinarian and the only doctor I know who can make a diagnosis without asking questions."

Wheeling and Dealing

A CONTRACTOR, hoping to grease the skids for a deal, asked the government agent if he'd like a nice foreign sports car.

"I can't accept a big expensive gift like that," the agent said indignantly. "It's a bribe!"

"Well, would it be all right if I sold you the car?" the contractor asked.

"For how much?" the agent said.

"Ten dollars," the contractor replied.

"In that case," the agent said, "I'll take two."

Now That Figures

A PATIENT was worried and pressed the doctor about his diagnosis.

"Are you sure it's pneumonia?" he asked. "I've heard of cases where a doctor treated a patient for pneumonia, and the patient ended up dying of something else."

"Not to worry," the doctor assured him. "When I treat a patient for pneumonia, he dies of pneumonia."

Ups and Downs

THERE'S AN ELEVATOR between Heaven and Hades, and it's the Devil's responsibility to keep it running. One day, after the elevator had broken down for the umpteenth time, God's patience ran out.

"Devil," the Lord said, "if you don't get that elevator running and keep it running, I'm going to sue you."

"You've got to be kidding," the Devil scoffed. "Where will you find a lawyer up there?"

So Many to Choose

THE PARENTS of a 5-year-old boy were curious about what career he'd pursue—law, banking, medicine or the clergy. A friend told them to put him alone in a room with a cigar, a dollar bill, a lollipop and a Bible. The item the child chose would indicate his calling.

When the boy came out of the room, he was sucking the lollipop, sniffing the cigar, tucking the dollar bill into his pocket and holding the Bible under one arm. "Oh, no!" the family friend gasped. "He's going to be a politician!"
—*Lola Heyl*
Cincinnati, Iowa

It's a Dog's Life

A PATIENT told his doctor, "This hospital is no good. You treat us like dogs."

"Mr. Jones, you know that's not true," the doctor replied. "Now roll over."

Flat Broke

THE PRISONER stood before the judge, awaiting sentencing on his conviction. "Have you anything to offer this court before I pass sentence?"

"Nope," the prisoner said. "My lawyer took every last penny."

Necessary Procedure

HAVE YOU HEARD about the doctor who doesn't believe in unnecessary surgery? He won't operate unless he really needs the money.

Sorry, Wrong Number

YOUNG DR. MALONEY hung out his shingle for the first time on Monday morning, but not a single patient showed up.

A week later, a man finally came to the office. In an attempt to impress him, Dr. Maloney picked up the phone and barked, "I have so many patients waiting, I don't think I'll be able to get to the hospital to perform brain surgery before 4."

The doctor hung up and turned to the visitor with a

"Or to put it another way, three times six plus two equals twenty."

smile. "And what seems to be paining you, my good man?" he asked.

"Nothing is paining me," the bewildered man said. "I just came to hook up your phone."

A Slip of the Tongue

ABRAHAM LINCOLN once told a story about an argument between a lawyer and a minister. "Do you ever make mistakes in court?" the minister asked.

"Very rarely," the lawyer sniffed.

"And what do you do when you make a mistake?" the minister asked.

"If they're large mistakes, I mend them," the lawyer said. "If they're small, I let them go. Don't you ever make mistakes while preaching?"

"Of course," the minister said. "And I dispose of them in the same way you do. Not long ago, I meant to tell the congregation that the Devil was the father of liars, but I made a mistake and said 'the father of lawyers'. The mistake was so small that I let it go."

"Besides showing you our dealer's invoice, here's a notarized statement from the manufacturer that *they* are losing money, too."

A Mighty Deep Subject

A GUIDE at the Grand Canyon stretched his arms wide and shouted, "It took *millions* of years to carve out this hole." One tourist muttered under his breath, "I'll bet it was a government job."
—*Tom Keegan Wamego, Kansas*

Swimming with Sharks

A DOCTOR, a minister and a lawyer huddled together in a tiny lifeboat. The water around them was filled with sharks.

Suddenly the lifeboat began to fill with water. As they furiously bailed, they noticed a sign on the boat that read: "Maximum capacity, two persons". They decided to draw straws to see who'd jump overboard.

The lawyer drew the short straw and promptly jumped into the water. As he swam away, the sharks didn't attack. Instead, they drew back to make a path for him.

Amazed, the doctor turned to the minister and exclaimed, "Surely this is a miracle!"

"That's no miracle," the minister responded. "Just professional courtesy."

No Speeches, Please

IN PIONEER DAYS, a young fellow was caught stealing horses. He was quickly tried and condemned to hang.

The sheriff put the noose around his neck and told him he could have 10 minutes to say anything he wanted. The young man declined.

Then the mayor offered to use up the 10 minutes with a speech. Asked if that would be all right, the horse thief answered, "I guess so. But I'd rather you hang me first."

Received a Promotion

A MAN visiting a school learned its mascot was a beloved hound dog called "Principal". When the visitor asked about the dog's name, a student explained, "Well, we call him that because he just weaves in and out of the rooms all day."

Several years later, the man returned and saw the same dog—but now everyone called it "Superintendent". The visitor asked why.

"Oh," a student replied, "he's pretty old now and doesn't get around much. He just sits in one spot and howls."

Scientific Advances

A PATIENT told her doctor she couldn't sleep at night. The doctor advised her to eat something before going to bed.

"But, Doctor," the woman objected, "2 months ago you told me to never eat anything before going to bed."

The doctor blinked and announced, "Why, my dear woman, that was 2 months ago. Science has made enormous strides since then."

Ouch, That Hurts

A WOMAN phoned her dentist after receiving an exorbitant bill.

"I'm shocked," she said. "This is three times what you normally charge."

"Yes, I know," the dentist replied. "But you yelled so loudly, you scared two other patients away."

Tested His Mettle

AT A UNIVERSITY, 1,000 students gathered in a large lecture hall for their final calculus exam. Throughout the test, the unpopular professor kept yelling out how much time they had left.

One student desperately needed a good grade to pass, but did poorly when rushed. When the professor announced, "Time's up", the student kept working. The other students filed forward and put their exams in a huge stack on the professor's desk.

Almost an hour after the test had officially ended, the student walked to the front of the room to submit his exam to the waiting professor.

"What do you think you're doing?" the professor barked.

"Turning in my exam," the student said.

"I have some bad news for you," the professor gloated. "Your exam is an hour late. You've failed it. I'll see you next term when you repeat my course."

The student smiled and asked, "Do you know who I am?"

"What?" the professor huffed.

"Do you know what my name is?"

"No, I don't," the professor snarled.

The student looked him in the eye and said, "I didn't think so." Then he lifted up the stack of exams, shoved his test neatly in the middle and walked out.

—Libby Wiebel
DePere, Wisconsin

Free Advice

A YOUNG DOCTOR complained to an older colleague, "Every time I attend my service club meetings, somebody gets me in the corner and starts pumping me for free medical advice. It's embarrassing, and I don't know how to stop it."

"No problem," the old-timer said. "I figured that out years ago. When somebody does that to me, I stop them with one word: 'undress'."

Important Work

A LAWYER was talking to his son about college. "I assume you plan to follow my profession and study law," he said.

"Not really, Dad," his son said. "I've given this a lot of thought, and I'd rather study medicine. Doctors are more important than lawyers."

His father was outraged. "Doctors more important than lawyers?" he shouted. "Where did you get such a stupid idea?"

"It's not so stupid," his son said. "Did you ever hear anybody at a football game stand up and shout, 'Is there a lawyer in the house'?"

He's Got a Point There

ABRAHAM LINCOLN was once accused during a debate of being two-faced. He replied, "I leave it to my audience—if I had two faces, would I be wearing this one?"

I'll Handle This

THE VICTIM of an automobile accident was lying in the street, badly injured. As a crowd gathered, a woman rushed over to the man and began to help him.

She was pushed aside almost instantly by a man who snapped, "Please step back and let me handle this. I've had a course in first aid."

The woman stood and watched the man work for a minute, then told him, "When you get to the part in your first-aid training where it says to call a doctor, don't bother. I'm already here."

That's Good News?

OLE went to the doctor for a checkup. Two days later, the nurse called and told him to come in right away. When he arrived, the doctor said, "I've got good news and bad news."

"Give me the good news first," Ole said.

"Well, you're going to die within 24 hours," the doctor said.

"If that's the *good* news, what's the bad news?"

The doctor said, "I was supposed to tell you yesterday."
—Don Meyer
Elma, Iowa

Brrrr!

DURING a bad cold spell, a man told his friend, "You know how cold it is? The other day I saw a politician on a street corner with his hands in *his own* pockets."

Radical Treatment

A YOUNG NUN bolted out of the doctor's office, weeping uncontrollably. A prominent Catholic layman witnessed the scene and barged in on the doctor, demanding to know what he'd said to so upset such a dear woman.

"I told her she was pregnant," the doctor said casually.

"Impossible!" the man raged. "Why would you do a thing like that?"

The doctor shrugged and said, "It sure stopped her hiccups."

Money Woes

"I'M ALWAYS worried about money," the patient told his psychiatrist.

"Not unusual, not at all," the expert said soothingly. "I can help you overcome that worry. But it's going to cost you plenty."

PSYCHIATRIST

" SATISFACTION GUARANTEED OR YOUR MANIA BACK"

Enter

Now, Walk The Plank!

A BANKER was chatting with a friend at the weekly meeting of their civic club. "When I was a little fellow," the banker said, "my ambition was to become a pirate."

"You must be quite happy," his friend said. "Few men ever realize their childhood dreams."

Ins and Outs

A FELLOW went to the doctor for a physical examination. The doctor found him fit as a fiddle, with no sign of any ailments. But when the man left the office, he dropped dead right outside the door.

The nurse ran in and told the doctor, "That man you just examined fell dead on his way out! What shall we do?"

The doctor replied, "Go out and turn him around so it looks like he's coming in."

—*Helene Notestine*
LaGrange, Indiana

Just a Figure Of Speech

THE DOCTOR was making a house call. "It's mighty nice of you to come all the way out here to see me," the patient said.

"Oh, don't mention it," the doctor replied. "I had another patient in this part of town, so I decided to kill two birds with one stone."

Let Us Pray

DURING a tour of the Capitol, the tour guide pointed to a tall man and said, "He's the congressional chaplain."

One tourist asked, "What does he do? Does he pray for the Senate or the House?"

"No," the guide said. "He gets up, looks at the Congress, then fervently prays for the country."

—*Joseph Orban*
Spring Hill, Florida

Ups and Downs Of Farming

A 90-year-old man asked his banker for a loan so he could buy some cattle. "Fine," the banker said, "you have a lot of collateral." But when he handed the note to the farmer, it was for only 6 months.

"I wanted this note for 10 years," the farmer protested.

The banker said, "Look, you're 90 years old. What if something happens to you?"

"Don't worry," the farmer said. "I hear things are nice in Heaven, so I can surely get the money back to you."

"But what if you go the other way?" the banker asked.

The farmer replied, "That's no problem. Then I'll just hand it to you."

—*Wendell Mueller*
Gilman, Illinois

That's a Long Day

THE POLITICIAN and his wife arrived home very late and fell onto the sofa, exhausted. "Oh, am I tired," the politician groaned. "This has been some day!"

"Me, too," his wife said. "I can't remember when I've been so tired."

"*You're* tired?" her husband asked. "I'm the one who made seven speeches today. Why are you so tired?"

"Because I had to listen to them."

Tripartite Truth

WASHINGTON is made of equal parts protocol, Geritol and know-it-all.

—*Tom Thieding*
Madison, Wisconsin

An Expert Observation

AN EFFICIENCY EXPERT walked into an office and asked the first clerk he met, "What do you do here?"

"Nothing," answered the clerk.

The expert nodded, made a note, then asked a second clerk, "And you, what is your job here?"

"I don't do anything, either," the clerk replied.

"Hmmm," the expert said. "Duplication."

In the Beginning...

HUNDREDS of top scientists worked together to build the ultimate computer—a master brain with the intellect to answer every question and solve all the mysteries of the world.

Finally the machine was completed and ready for its first question. With trembling hands, a scientist fed in the query: "How did the world start?"

Lights flashed, wheels whirred, tumblers clicked. Then the machine answered: "See Genesis 1:1."

What's Ailing You?

A MAN walked into a doctor's office. The receptionist asked him what he had. "Shingles," he said. The receptionist took down his name, phone number and

"When people ask me what I do, I tell them I'm a topnotch banker."

insurance information and told him to have a seat.

Fifteen minutes later, a nurse's aide took the man to an examining room and asked what he had. "Shingles," he said. The aide took his height, weight and medical history, then told him to wait.

Half an hour later, a nurse came in and asked the man what he had. "Shingles," he said. The nurse took his blood pressure and told him to undress and wait for the doctor.

An hour later, the doctor came in and asked the man what he had. "Shingles," the man said.

"Where?" the doctor asked.

"Outside in the truck," the man said. "Where do you want them?"

—*Margaret Buechel Malone, Wisconsin*

"Remember, Slim — efficiency, efficiency."

The Fix is In

GOD ASKED St. Peter to refurbish the Pearly Gates, so the saint began interviewing applicants for the job. "I used to be a carpenter," the first man said. "I could fix those gates for $500."

"I'll think it over and get back to you," St. Peter said.

The second man said, "I used to be a general contractor. I can have someone fix those gates for you for only $5,000."

"That sounds kind of steep," St. Peter said. "I'll get back to you."

The next applicant said, "I used to be a government contractor. I can have somebody fix those gates for you for $20,500."

"You must be kidding," St. Peter exclaimed. "That's outrageous!"

"No it isn't," the man replied. "That's $10,000 for you, $10,000 for me and $500 for the carpenter over there to do the job."

Used Parts

ONE DAY a tourist in Washington came across a walk-in brain-transplant business. He was told he could get a farmer's brain for $500, a lawyer's for $1,000 or a congressman's for $5,000.

"Why does it cost less to have a farmer's brain than a congressman's brain?" the tourist asked.

"That's simple," the surgeon said. "The congressman's brain has never been used." —*Tom Thieding*
Madison, Wisconsin

Think About This

THE JUDGE asked a man on the witness stand to tell what he knew about the case. The witness began, "I think…"

"Hold on!" the judge interrupted him. "We don't want you to think. We want you to tell us the facts."

"I understand, Judge," the witness said. "But I'm no lawyer. I can't talk without thinking."

Baaad Math

AN ECONOMIST was walking along a country road when he saw a shepherd and decided to have a little fun.

He said to the shepherd, "If I can tell you exactly how many sheep are in your flock, can I have one?"

The shepherd felt pretty confident the fellow couldn't guess correctly, so he said, "Sure".

The economist made a mental calculation of the number of sheep in a square yard and the size of the barnyard and announced, "Nine hundred seventy-three sheep."

Dismayed, the shepherd watched the economist grab an animal and start walking away.

"Wait just a minute," the shepherd called after the man. "Let's go double or nothing. I'll bet that I can tell you what you do for a living."

"You're on," the economist said.

"You work for one of those think tanks in Washington, D.C."

The startled economist asked, "How did you know that?"

The shepherd replied, "I'll tell you as soon as you release my dog."
—*Howard Rand*
Marshfield, Wisconsin

The Check Came Back

A COUNTRY DOCTOR met a patient whose check had bounced. Trying to be tactful, the doctor said, "By the way, your check came back."

"What a coincidence," the farmer drawled. "So did my lumbago."

Who Invited the Radiologist?

A FRIEND was dressing her two children for Halloween. The 4-year-old was costumed as a pumpkin, and her 10-month-old brother wore a black sweat suit imprinted with a skeleton design.

Their mother asked the 4-year-old, "Do you know what your little brother is?"

"Yes," the big sister said. "He's an X-ray."
—Mary Kay Lane
Muscatine, Iowa

Making Payments

"AFTER YOUR SURGERY," the doctor said, "you can pay $500 down and $300 a month."

"But that's like buying a new car," the patient said.

"You're right," the doctor replied. "I am."

Hot and Dry

WHILE visiting Washington, I saw this sign in the bathroom of a congressional office building, next to the hot-air hand dryer: "To speak to your congressman, push button."
—Tom Thieding
Madison, Wisconsin

All in Favor...

TWO MEMBERS of the Town Council got into a shouting match during a meeting.

"You are the biggest idiot in the world," the first man yelled.

"And you're the most bigoted jerk in the world," the second retorted.

The mayor, who was presiding over the meeting, banged his gavel and said, "Quiet, gentlemen. I'm afraid that in your excitement you've forgotten that I am in the room."

Now He *Really* Needs Help

THE NEW EMPLOYEE stood before the paper shredder, looking confused.

"Need some help?" a passing secretary asked.

"Yes," the new man replied. "How does this thing work?"

"It's easy," the secretary said, taking the report from his hands and feeding it into the shredder.

Puzzled, the man said, "Thanks. But where do the copies come out?"

Hoofing It

BILL WENT to see the doctor for a leg injury. "No need to worry," the physician assured him. "I'll have you walking in a few days."

"Man, was he right," Bill moaned later. "I had to sell my car to pay his bill."

"I'll pay it! How much?"

Proud Pooch

A WOMAN visited a kennel to select a dog. "I want a dog I can be proud of," she told the owner. "Does that one have a good pedigree?"

"Lady," the owner said, "if he could talk, he wouldn't speak to either of us."

The Knee Bone's Connected to the...

MY 5-year-old nephew and I were watching a science program on television that showed a human skeleton.

"Do you know what a skeleton is?" I asked the child.

"Yes," he replied. "It's a bunch of bones with the person off." —J. Hampsch
Los Angeles, California

Ethics in Government

A CONGRESSMAN'S wife woke in the middle of the night and heard intruders moving through the rooms downstairs. Frantic, she shook her husband and whispered hoarsely, "There are crooks in the house!"

"That may be true," her husband answered drowsily, "but those guys in the Senate aren't all angels, either."

Wrong Turn

A MOTORIST lost control of his car and ran up onto the porch of a roadside cottage.

Embarrassed, the man climbed out of his car and mumbled to the lady of the house, "Can you tell me the way to Farmingdale?"

The woman replied coldly, "Straight ahead through the living room, and turn left at the pantry."

That's What They All Say

THE NEWSPAPER office boy was having trouble with all the visitors demanding to see the editor. "I can't keep them away," the boy told his boss. "When I say you're out, they don't believe me and say they *must* see you."

The editor replied, "Just tell them, 'That's what they all say'. I don't care if you offend them. I cannot be disturbed."

That afternoon, a lady

called at the office and asked to see the editor. The office boy told her that was impossible.

"But I must see him," the woman protested. "I'm his wife."

"That's what they all say," the office boy replied.

Better Iron This Out

WHEN ASKED what she'd like for breakfast, our 4-year-old granddaughter said, "Waffles. Do you know how to make them?"

"Yes," I said, "but I don't have a waffle iron."

She replied in a shocked tone, "Grandma, you don't iron waffles. You pop them in a toaster."

—*Ida Mae Behrend*
Colesburg, Iowa

The Voice of Experience

A RETIRED NEIGHBOR took his 5-year-old grandson along on a shopping trip. When Grandpa found a fishing pole he admired, he showed it to his grandson. "Oh, Jimmy," he said, "I wish I could get one of these."

"Cry a little bit when you tell Grammy about it," Jimmy advised. "Then she'll let you buy it."

—*Stella Reed*
Freemansburg,
Pennsylvania

Executive Ability

A YOUNGSTER overheard a group of grown-ups talking about the business world. Later, he asked his father, "What's executive ability?"

"My son, that's the art of getting the credit for all the hard work that somebody else does."

Alarming Advice

"DOCTOR, every night I dream that I'm being chased by a creature from outer space," the worried patient said.

"Just when it's about to catch me, the alarm clock goes off, I wake up, and I'm safe and sound. What's your advice?"

"Don't forget to set the alarm."

Chapter Three

Family Fun

A good sense of
humor never fails to
pull family members
closer together.
Come share the fun.

Watch This Shot!

A GOLFER told his caddie, "I'm eager to make this shot. That's my mother-in-law up there on the clubhouse porch."

"That's over 300 yards," the caddie said doubtfully. "You'll never hit her from here."

Getting Punchy

AT A NEW YEAR'S Eve party, a woman whispered to her husband, "That's the fifth time you've gone back for more punch. Doesn't it embarrass you a little?"

"Not at all," he grinned. "I keep telling them it's for you."

Wedded Bliss

GRANDMA and Grandpa had a busy day on their 50th wedding anniversary, with many well-wishers stopping by to offer congratulations. When all the guests had gone home and the two were settled in their recliners, Grandpa said, "Mother, I'm proud of you."

"What's that you say?" she asked. "You know I can't hear you without my hearing aid."

"I said, 'I'm proud of you'."

"That's all right," Grandma murmured, "I'm tired of you, too."

All in the Family

THE STUDENTS at an all-girls' college were allowed to date only on Saturday nights.

One Tuesday evening, a young man showed up and told an older woman in the dormitory lobby it was imperative he see a certain young lady immediately.

"I want to surprise her," the young man said. "You see, I'm her brother."

"Oh, she'll be surprised all right," the woman replied. "But think of how surprised *I* am. I'm her mother."

Dressed for The Occasion

A WOMAN waited until her husband had finished supper and was settled into his chair in front of the TV set. Then she changed into a cocktail dress and paraded before him.

"How do you like my new dress?" she asked. "I think it'll be just the thing to wear to the cocktail party next week."

"Take it back," her husband said. "It's terrible. I wouldn't want to be seen at the party with you in that dress."

"That's just what I hoped you'd say," she agreed.

"This is my old cocktail dress. Now I can go buy a new one. Thanks, darling."

Make It Yourself

A MAN asked his wife, "What would you like for Christmas?"

"Nothing much," she replied. "How about something you made yourself—like money?"

"This is what makes marriage fun, doing things together."

"The credit card company may call it a 'cash advance', but to us it's a cash *retreat*."

Out of Tune

LITTLE SAMMY was practicing his violin while his father tried to read the paper in another room. The family dog was lying at the man's feet.

As the screeching sound of the violin reached the dog's ears, the pup began to howl dismally.

The father endured this racket as long as he could. Finally, he threw his paper to the floor and yelled above the din, "For heaven's sake, can't you play something the dog doesn't know?"

Another Lost Opportunity

THREE construction workers were killed in a fall from a skyscraper. A fourth worker told his wife, "It was just terrible. But their widows are getting $2,000 a month."

"That's just like you," his wife exclaimed. "Whenever there's a chance to make some money, you're not there."

What Was Your Name Again?

A GI STATIONED in Germany received a "Dear John" letter from his sweetheart. She was going to marry a sailor and wanted him to return the photo she'd given him.

The GI's buddies collected photos from every soldier they knew and shipped a huge crate of them to the fickle girl. When she opened the crate, she found this note: "Please pick out your picture and return the rest to me. I don't remember which one is yours."

Recipe for Disaster

"SURELY," the marriage counselor insisted, "you must have said something to start such a terrible argument."

"Not really," the husband said. "My wife had tried a new recipe for dinner. When she asked how I liked it, all I said was, 'It's okay, but it'll never take the place of food'."

Back-Seat Driver

A POLICE OFFICER stopped a motorist on the highway. "Sir," the officer told the driver, "didn't you realize your wife fell out of the car about a mile back?"

"Thank goodness!" the driver replied. "I thought I'd gone deaf."

Thinking Alike

"DOES your boyfriend have any money?" a man asked his daughter.

"You men all think alike," she said. "That's exactly what he asked about you."

Look Me Up

"IF YOU give me your telephone number, I'll call you up sometime," the hopeful young man told a young lady.

"It's in the telephone book," she replied.

"Great!" the man said. "What's your name?"

"That's in the book, too."

Off to a Bad Start

A DOCTOR was treating a woman for depression. Trying to learn more about her symptoms, he asked, "How do you start your day? Do you wake up grumpy?"

"No, sir," she snapped. "I just let him sleep."

Lots of Hot Air

A WOMAN told her friend about her plans to visit Yellowstone National Park. "Don't forget Old Faithful," her friend said.

"Oh, I won't," the lady replied. "He's going with me."

Let the Punishment Fit the Crime

A WOMAN was being questioned in court about serving on a jury. "I'm sorry, Your Honor," she told the judge. "I can't serve on this jury. I don't believe in capital punishment."

"Maybe you don't understand," the judge said. "This is a civil suit brought by a woman to recover $5,000 her husband spent on gambling and other women."

"Oh," the woman said. "In that case, I'd be happy to serve. I could be wrong about capital punishment."

Distant Memories

DURING A PAUSE at the bridge table, one woman addressed the hostess, "I suppose you carry some sort of memento in that locket you're wearing."

"Yes, it's a lock of my husband's hair," the hostess replied.

"But your husband's still alive!"

"Of course," the hostess agreed. "But his hair is gone."

Repeat After Me...

THE ENGLISH PROFESSOR was trying to impress his class with the importance of a large vocabulary. "I assure you," he said, "if you repeat a word 10 or 12 times, it will be yours forever."

A girl in the back of the room took a deep breath, closed her eyes and whispered, "Robert, Robert, Robert..."

Really Burned Them Up

TWO unmarried sisters were

"Is this really necessary? Couldn't we just read him a bedtime story?"

spending a typical evening at home together.

Suddenly one looked up from her newspaper and said, "Listen to this. Here's a story about a woman who was married four times. Each time her husband died, and each time she had him cremated."

"That's the way it goes," her sister said. "Here we are with no husbands and that woman has husbands to burn."

Friend of The Bride?

THE WEDDING USHERS were instructed to seat the friends of the bride on one side and friends of the groom on the other.

As one woman entered the sanctuary, an usher asked, "Are you a friend of the bride?"

The lady quickly replied, "Good heavens, no! I'm the groom's mother."

That's a Valid Reason

TWO EXPLORERS camped in the heart of an African jungle were discussing their expedition.

"I came here because the urge to travel was in my blood," one said. "The dullness of city life bored me. I wanted to see the sun rise over new horizons and hear the flutter of birds that had never been scared by man. I wanted to leave my footprints on sand unmarked before I came. In short, I wanted to see nature in all its splendor. Why did you come?"

The second explorer replied, "My son was taking saxophone lessons."

"Aren't you getting a little carried away on this economy kick?"

Waiting for Mr. Right

"OUR DAUGHTER will be 26 next month," a woman reminded her husband. "Don't you think it's time she got married?"

"Oh, there's no hurry, dear," her husband replied. "Better let her wait until the right man comes along."

"Why should she wait?" his wife objected. "I didn't."

How Sweet the Sound?

UNCLE WILBUR asked that Aunt Agatha sing *Amazing Grace* at his funeral. He always claimed his wife's singing could wake the dead and figured it was worth a try.

Proud of His Heritage

WILL ROGERS had just spoken to a group of society ladies who clearly considered themselves superior to average folks. One woman managed to get his attention and then declared proudly, "My ancestors came over on the *Mayflower*."

Rogers, who was part Native American, grinned and replied, "My ancestors met the boat."

A Peaceful Night at Home

AS A COUPLE pulled into their driveway after an evening away at the movies, they could hear the stereo blasting away inside the house.

They walked in and found their teenage son sitting in front of the throbbing speakers with a book in his hands.

The father turned down the stereo and asked the teen what he'd been doing all evening.

"Nothing much," the youth replied, "just enjoying the peace and quiet of being home alone."

Fully Covered

A MINISTER went to see a woman whose husband had just passed away. "Was your husband covered by insurance?" the clergyman inquired.

"Oh, no," the widow replied. "Just his nightshirt."

What are Your Intentions?

A CAGEY FELLOW had been calling on the same girl for 3 years. Though he seemed genuinely fond of her, he never even hinted at marriage.

The girl's parents, anxious to see her happily married, were concerned that this fellow took up so much of her time that she couldn't see anyone else.

"I've had enough of this," her father finally said. "He and I are going to have a talk."

When the suitor called later that night, the girl's father said, "Young man, you've been calling on my daughter for 3 years. I want to know—are your intentions honorable or dishonorable?"

The fellow said, "You mean I've got a choice?"

Maybe She's Right

THE MINISTER asked the groom, "Do you take this woman for better, for worse; for richer, for poorer; in sickness and in health; through good times and bad?"

"Wait a minute, Preach- er," the bride interrupted. "You're going to talk him right out of it!"

A Born Accountant

THE BRIDE-TO-BE was addressing her wedding invitations. Her mother noticed she'd invited only married couples. "Why aren't you inviting any of your single friends?" she asked.

"If I invite unmarried people, someday I'll have to return the favor and buy wedding presents for them," her daughter replied. "This way, all our presents will be clear profit."

Foolish Talk

A MAN told his wife, "I was a fool when I married you."

"I know," she replied. "But I thought you'd get over it."

How's That Again?

AT A FUNERAL, the preacher talked on and on about the deceased's fine qualities—good husband, upstanding citizen, wonderful father, devout Christian. The man's widow whispered to her oldest son, "Go up there and see if that's your daddy. I believe they've got the wrong man in the casket."

In Plain English

THE ANXIOUS PATIENT told his doctor, "If there's anything wrong with me, don't frighten me half to death by giving it a long scientific name. Just tell me what it is in plain English."

"Well, sir, to be frank, you're lazy."

"Thank you, Doctor," the man said. "Now tell me the scientific name for that. I've got to report back to the missus."

Reluctant Bride

A MINISTER went to a prospective bride's home to discuss the wedding with her family. At one point, the would-be bride said, "But, Father, I don't want to leave Mother!"

"Well, don't let me stand in the way of your happiness," her father said. "Take your mother with you."

You Can Forget It!

EDDIE had such a miserable toothache he thought he was going to die. "What can I do to relieve this suffering?" he asked a friend.

"I'll tell you what I do," his friend said. "When I have a toothache, or any other kind of pain, I go to my wife. She puts her arms around me and caresses and soothes me until I forget all about the pain."

"Gee, that sounds like a wonderful idea," Eddie said. "Is she home now?"

Handyman Wanted

A MINISTER put an ad in the paper for a handyman. The next morning, a well-dressed young man came to the door.

"Can you start a fire and have breakfast ready by 7 a.m.?" the minister asked.

The young man said he thought he could.

"Can you polish the silver, wash the dishes, keep the place picked up and mow the lawn?" the minister continued.

"Look," the young man said. "I came to make arrangements for my wedding, but if it's going to be like that, let's just forget the whole thing."

Contract Sport

A MAN WALKED into a bookstore, unaware that it was a specialty shop with a limited range of subjects. "I'm looking for a book on bridge," he told the owner.

"I'm sorry," the owner said. "We only sell science fiction and fantasy."

The man grinned and replied, "You've never seen my wife play bridge."

Don't Forget to Write

TWO FATHERS were discussing how their sons were doing in college. One man said, "My son is so smart that when he writes home, I have to go to the dictionary."

"You're lucky," the other father sighed. "When my son writes home, I have to go to the bank."

No Complaints Here

DANIEL was married to a wonderful woman, but his mother-in-law was a holy terror. After the older woman passed away, the priest stopped by to offer condolences.

"What complaint did your mother-in-law die of, Daniel?" the priest asked sympathetically.

"Well, Father," Daniel replied, "there wasn't any complaint. Everybody was satisfied."

Just Like Magic

"MY HUSBAND, Stanley, and I enjoy a magical relationship," Maude told her friend. "Whenever I ask him to do something for me, he disappears."

Man or Beast?

A TEENAGE GIRL watched unhappily as her mother tried on a new fur coat. "Mom," she said, "do you realize some poor dumb beast suffered so you could buy that coat?"

The woman looked at her daughter sternly and scolded, "Don't talk about your father that way."

Now That Makes Scents

AS MY HUSBAND and I prepared for an evening out, I sprayed on a little fragrance. Our 5-year-old was watching and asked what it was.

I turned toward him with the atomizer and said, "Perfume. Do you want some?"

He quickly backed away, protesting, "No, I don't want to be perfumigated!"

—*Mrs. Eugene Born*
Sequim, Washington

Monster Alert

MY 6-year-old nephew woke from a nightmare and began calling for his mother. "There's a monster under my bed, Mommy!" he exclaimed.

My sister looked under the bed and found nothing but an accumulation of little-boy treasures. She assured him he needn't worry, because no monster could possibly fit under there.

Without hesitation, he replied earnestly, "It's a *flat* monster, Mom."

—*Donna Giger*
Trenton, Illinois

What Could Be Worse?

"IT COULD BE worse." That's what the man said, no matter what happened or how bad it was. His sons heard this phrase so often they grew tired of it.

One morning, the boys told their father they'd dreamed he died and went to...well, not Heaven.

"It could be worse," their father replied.

The boys couldn't believe their ears. "What could be worse than that?" they asked.

"It could be true," their father said.

—*William Bourque*
Oklee, Minnesota

Bearing Gifts

AN OLDER MAN was talking with a young man who was about to be married.

"When you give gifts to your wife, you'll find that she goes through three stages," the older man said. "When you're first married, she'll say, 'You're the sweetest, most wonderful husband in the world'.

"Then, before you know it, she'll accept a gift with, 'Well, it's about time. I thought you'd never get it for me'."

"And what's the third stage?" the young man asked.

The old man sighed. "That's when she says to herself, 'He gave me this without a struggle. I wonder what he's up to'."

How Big Is That House?

I WAS PREGNANT (over-due, in fact) and baby-sitting for my 11-year-old brother. As we finished a game, he helped me up off the floor and asked if I was ready for the baby to arrive.

"I sure am," I said, struggling to my feet. "I feel big as a house."

He considered this, then said innocently, "Don't you mean a *boarding house*?"

I laughed so hard I nearly went into labor.

—Connie Hughes
Penrose, Colorado

Having a Father-Son Talk

A FATHER was convinced the younger generation was

"No, you may *not* have one of my biscuits
to use for a hockey puck."

not as industrious as his own.

"Son," he said, "when Abraham Lincoln was your age he was out splitting rails."

"Yes, I've read about that, Dad," his son replied. "And when he was your age he was president."

All the Kinfolks Gathered 'Round

MY 4-year-old son and I were walking along a boulevard lined with stylish shops. When I stopped to admire a window display of dresses, Alan peered at it and asked, "Is that a real live person in there?"

"No," I explained, "it's a statue called a mannequin."

Alan responded, "It looks like a ladykin to me."

—Barbara Mallery
Santa Fe, New Mexico

Opposite View

A MAN advised his son to marry someone with similar interests, religious beliefs and ideals.

"Oh, Dad," the younger man said. "You're living in the dark ages. Don't you know that opposites attract?"

"Listen, son," his father shot back, "just being boy and girl is opposite enough."

Sub-Standard Wage

A JOB-SEEKER walked in the house and announced, "Honey, I got a job!"

"Great!" she said. "What's the pay?"

"Oh, they said they'll pay me what I'm worth."

"What?" his wife sputtered. "We can't live on that!"

Hug the Cook

MY 7-year-old granddaughter was sitting on the kitchen counter as we baked cookies together. I gave her a big hug and told her I was sad she was growing up so fast and that our fun times would eventually come to an end.

Erin gave me a big hug in return and said, "Don't worry, Grandma. You'll always be able to cook for me."
—Bess Massingham
Eugene, Oregon

Question Made Her Day

ONE EVENING, my second-grade son was doing his homework and asked, "Mom, how do you spell 'maid'?"

"M-A-D-E," I replied.

"No," he said. "I mean 'maid'—like a wife."

—Terri Trierweiler
Portland, Michigan

A Logical Response

"I KNOW why some women are called drop-dead gorgeous," a bachelor told his buddy.

"Why?"

"Because whenever I ask one of them out, she tells me to drop dead."

Have a Safe Trip

A TEENAGER had just received her learner's permit and offered to drive her parents to church. After a long rough ride, they finally reached their destination. The driver's mother got out of the car and said, "Thank you."

"Anytime," her teenager replied.

As the woman slammed the door, she said, "I wasn't talking to you. I was talking to God."

No Receipt, No Return

MY NIECE was returning a new pair of Easter shoes at a department store. When the clerk asked for her receipt, my niece's little son piped up, "The Easter rabbit doesn't give receipts."

—Ruth Freeman
Pillager, Minnesota

Christmas Wish

IT WAS CHRISTMAS eve, and two unmarried sisters were planning their holiday.

The older sister said, "Well, it's time to hang up our stockings. Would a longer stocking hold what you'd like to have for Christmas?"

The younger one shook her head and murmured wistfully, "No, but a pair of socks would."

Proper Punctuation

MY 6-year-old grandson was in first grade and learning to read. One day he got into a dispute with his mother, who told him sternly, "Don't argue, just do it, period." The child immediately replied, "I think that should be an exclamation mark, Mom."

—Susan Petersen
Davenport, Iowa

"Ma, come make my snake give me back my frog!"

"When I was your age we didn't have videos with playback. I had to *remember* the plot."

Hard to Swallow

A YOUNG GIRL baked a cake as a surprise for her mother's birthday. The woman bravely gulped down a few bites, even though the cake was almost impossible to swallow, and tried to indicate she was enjoying it.

"I'm so glad you like it, Mommy," the little girl beamed. "There should've been 32 candles on the cake, but they were all gone when I took it out of the oven."

Getting to The Point

THE 8-year-old didn't mind going to church—it was the pastor's lengthy prayers that bored him. When his parents invited the pastor for dinner, the child was apprehensive.

To the child's relief, when

the pastor said grace he was quick and got right to the point.

Pleased, the child looked up at the reverend and said, "You don't pray so long when you're hungry, do you?"

A Whiz Kid

A WOMAN was quite proud of her son's scientific knowledge and wanted to show him off to her bridge club. She called him in and asked proudly, "Bobby, what does it mean when steam comes out of the teakettle spout?"

Bobby replied, "That you're going to open one of Daddy's letters."

Modern Discipline

A FRUSTRATED FATHER was telling a friend how difficult it was to punish a teenager.

"When I was a youngster," the man explained, "my father sent me to my room without supper. But my son has his own TV, stereo, phone and microwave oven."

"So what do you do?" his friend asked.

"Send him to my room."

Practice Makes Perfect

GRANDMOTHER was trying to teach little Tommy some table manners. After a few lessons, he said, "Grandmother, you said I should always eat my pie with a fork when I'm invited out to dinner."

"Yes, that's right," his grandmother replied.

"Well," Tommy said, "would you have a piece that I could practice on?"

Working Like A Dog

A BOY told his father he was going to rake leaves in the neighborhood to earn some money. A short time later, he came home with $100 to put in the bank.

"Well, well," said his father, pleasantly surprised. "You raked a lot of leaves, son."

"Just one yard, Dad," the boy replied. "And their dog bit me."

Chapter Four

No Chuckling In Church!

The clergy and
their faithful flock
can be as quick
with a joke as any
good comedian.
Read on...but no
laughing during
services.

Snappy Comeback

WHEN the new preacher moved to town, one of the first people he met said, "I certainly hope you're not one of those narrow-minded ministers who thinks only the members of their congregation are going to Heaven."

"I'm even more narrow-minded than that," the preacher replied. "I'm pretty sure some of the members of my congregation aren't going to make it, either."

That's Some Foursome

JESUS and Moses were golfing in Heaven and came to a water hazard. Moses' ball headed straight for the water, but the water parted and the ball rolled across dry land to the green.

Jesus' ball went toward the water, too, but stopped on top. Jesus walked across the water and played through.

When a third fellow in their party took his turn, his ball landed on a lily pad. A frog jumped up and grabbed the ball in its mouth. Then an eagle swooped down, picked up the frog and flew over the green. The frog dropped the ball into the cup for a hole-in-one.

Moses shook his head, turned to Jesus, and said, "That's what I hate about playing with your dad."
—*Dee Arnold*
Springfield, Missouri

Well-Minced Words

AT CHRISTMAS, the minister's family received a mince pie from a woman who was a devoted churchgoer but a very poor cook. The pie was so spicy and dry the family had to throw it out.

In an attempt to be truthful when thanking this kind-hearted cook, the minister said, "We appreciate your gift, and let me assure you that a mince pie like yours never lasts long at our house."

Take Your Pick

TWO American ministers visited a church while traveling in Germany. They couldn't speak German, so they decided to sit behind a dignified-looking gentleman and do whatever he did.

During the service, the pastor made a special announcement, and the man in front of them rose. The Americans quickly jumped to their feet, only to be met by roars of laughter. The Americans later went to shake the pastor's hand. When they learned he spoke English, they asked what all the laughter was about.

"Oh," said the pastor, "I was announcing a baptism, and I asked the father of the child to stand."

—*Marilyn Ubben Williams, Iowa*

Get on Board!

SMITTY was a hard-headed man. When floodwaters surrounded his house, he climbed to the roof. A rescue boat came by, but Smitty refused their offer of help. "I have faith in the Lord," he called out. "He will save me."

The waves rose higher, and Smitty scrambled to the tip of his roof. Another rescue boat came by, but Smitty again refused help, saying the Lord would save him.

When the waves began to lap at his feet, Smitty pulled himself to the top of the chimney. A helicopter swooped down to rescue him, but Smitty waved it off. "The Lord will save me," he yelled. Of course, Smitty drowned.

When he stood before the Lord, Smitty complained, "Lord, I had such faith in you. Why didn't you save me?"

The Lord replied, "What more did you want? I sent you two boats and a helicopter!"

Which Way Is It?

A PREACHER was walking down the street, looking for the post office, when he noticed a young boy standing nearby. He walked over and told him, "Sonny, I'll give you a quarter if you could show me where the post office is."

The boy took the preacher to the post office. The preacher gave him the quarter, then said, "Sonny, I'll tell you how to get to Heaven if you come to Sunday school and church tomorrow." The boy looked the preacher in the eye and said, "I don't know about that—you couldn't find the post office."

—*Marie Birkner Pinckneyville, Illinois*

"It's true your father has served in a number of parishes, but you must stop describing yourself as 'a clergy brat'."

Was Moses a Pilot?

A LITTLE BOY returned home from Sunday school and told his mom he'd learned a story about the Egyptians chasing the Israelites to the Red Sea.

"Then," the boy concluded, "the Israelites called in a bunch of helicopters to get them across."

Astonished, his mother asked, "Aren't you adding to the stor?"

"Look, Mom," the boy said, "if I told you the story the teacher gave us, you'd *never* believe me."

—*Glenn Baker*
Clearwater, Florida

The Blessings Of Brevity

AT A RECENT church social, a well-known and long-winded preacher was about to begin his address. But first, the Master of Ceremonies called on Old Joe to return thanks.

"Dear Lord," Joe intoned,

"Your blessings are everlasting. Grant that the preacher's address will not be. Amen." —Art Ward
Salisbury, Maryland

It's a Barbecue!

OUR PASTOR was preaching about missing Sunday school and church. He cited the Bible story in which the Pharisees criticized Jesus for healing on the Sabbath. Jesus told them, "If a lamb falls into a pit, you should rescue him, even if it is on the Sabbath."

Our preacher added, "If that lamb falls into a pit three Sundays in a row, it's time to have lamb chops."
—Lloyd Sines
Findlay, Ohio

He's Celebrated In Song

A SUNDAY SCHOOL teacher asked her class to draw pictures of the Nativity scene. One child's version included the three wise men, plus a very fat man. Asked who the fourth man was, the child replied innocently, "Round John Virgin".
—Harley Schlabach
Arthur, Illinois

Talk to the Boss

A MINISTER and a salesman were seated side by side on an airplane that flew into a violent storm. The frightened salesman asked the minister, "Can't you do something to stop this storm?"

"Sorry, I can't," the preacher said.

"But you're a man of God," the salesman insisted.

"I know, I know," the minister said. "But I'm in sales, not management."

The Naked Truth

JOHNNY wanted to play ball on Sunday afternoon, but he knew his pastor father had a long sermon planned for that morning. So he quietly went to the pulpit and removed the last two pages of the sermon.

When the pastor got to the last page, he read, "And Adam said to Eve..." and stopped. The rest of the sermon was gone. Thinking he'd remember the rest of the sermon, he tried again. "And Adam said to Eve..." Still nothing.

Finally, the pastor said, "And Adam said to Eve, 'There must be a leaf missing here'." —Reinhart Besel
Saint James, Minnesota

Anything Not Nailed Down

A WORKER at a lumber-yard stole something every night before he went home—lumber, tools, nails, anything he could carry. After some time, he began to feel guilty and went to confession.

"Father," he said, "I stole."

"How much?" the priest asked.

"A lot," the man admitted.

"How much is a lot?"

"Enough to build a house."

The priest said, "This is very serious. For your penance you must make a novena."

The man said, "Good, Father. You get me the lumber, and I'll build you one."

—*Charles Mleziva*
Manitowoc, Wisconsin

The Best is Yet To Come?

THE PARISH was giving a farewell party for its priest. One dear old lady wept continuously as she shook hands with him. "I'm so sorry to see you go," she sobbed.

"Now, now, don't cry," the priest consoled her. "The bishop will send you a good pastor in my place. In fact, he'll send you a much better one."

At that, the woman wailed louder, "That's what they told me the last time!"

Parishioner, Heal Thyself

A GRAY-HAIRED WOMAN, a longtime member of her church, shook hands with the minister after Sunday services. "That was a wonderful sermon, just wonderful," she told him. "Everything you said applies to someone I know."

Rollin' Along

WHEN an old cat died and went to Heaven, God asked what He could do to make him more comfortable. "I'd like a soft pillow and a place to sleep in the sun," the cat said. His wish was granted.

A few days later, five mice died and went to Heaven, and God asked what they would like. "We'd like roller-skates, so we can get around better in such a big lovely place," they said. God gave them their wish.

Later, God ran into the cat and asked if he was happy. "Oh, yes, dear God," the cat said. "Everything is wonderful. And thank you so much for the delicious meals-on-wheels!" —*Emily Livangood Sparta, Wisconsin*

Short and Sweet

SOMEONE ONCE asked comedian George Burns what he considered a good sermon. He replied, "A good sermon should have a good beginning, a good ending, and they should be as close together as possible."

Anybody Home?

A MINISTER was talking to a poor parishioner who worked very hard as a cleaning lady. He said it was good to see her in church every Sunday, being so attentive to his sermons.

"Yes," she replied. "It's so restful after a week of hard work to come to church, sit down on soft cushions and not think about a thing."

The Wages of Sin?

ONE SUNDAY a student preacher came to a church in tobacco country and delivered a fire-and-brimstone sermon against tobacco use.

After the service, when it was time for the preacher to be paid, the church treasurer told him, "You ought to know, this money came from tobacco."

The preacher took a look at the money, then held out his hand and said, "Well, the Devil's had it long enough."
—*Adeline Tomesh Rice Lake, Wisconsin*

Pay Up, Folks

A YOUNG MAN asked his minister if there was something he could do for his church. The minister suggested he contact the members who had failed to send in the money they had pledged.

The next Sunday, the minister announced he had received quite a lot of money and some letters. One letter said, "Here's the money we failed to send, and you should tell your secretary there's only one 'R' in 'dirty' and no 'C' in 'skunk'."

Bagful of Wisdom

THE CHURCH CUSTODIAN was cleaning the sanctuary when he found a brown bag under one of the pews. He peeked inside, then went straight to the pastor's office.

"I think you should cut down on the length of your sermons," the custodian said.

"Why?" asked the pastor, taken aback.

"Look at this," the custodian said, holding out the bag. "People are starting to bring lunches."

handed down today, they'd be challenged in court for discriminating against sinners." —*Karen Ruthenbeck New Lenox, Illinois*

By the Board

DURING Sunday services, the minister announced there would be a meeting of the board after church. Much to his surprise, a visitor came to the meeting. Asked why, he replied, "I was as bored as everyone else." —*Richard Woody Crawfordsville, Indiana*

Pray Tell!

OUR granddaughter Lori had been watching a praying mantis in the yard for some time. Finally she ran into the house, yelling, "Mammaw, come quick! There's a praying minister out here!" —*Vivian Boyd Swords Creek, Virginia*

A Long Time To Wait

A MAN and a woman died in a car crash the day before their wedding. When they got to Heaven, St. Peter asked if there was anything he could do to make their stay more enjoyable. The couple asked if they could be married.

"Not right now," St. Peter said. "Come back in a year and we'll see."

A year passed, and the couple returned, again asking to be married. But St. Peter told them to come

Politically Incorrect

ONE PREACHER said to another, "You know, if the Ten Commandments were

"Do you have something lighter?
I like to hold my head up in church."

back in another year. This continued for 8 more years. After 10 years, he finally allowed them to marry.

Six months later, the couple returned to St. Peter with long faces. The husband said, "Now we understand why you made us wait so long. We can't stand each other and want a divorce."

St. Peter threw up his hands and said, "*Ten years* it took me to find you a preacher up here, and now you want me to find a *lawyer*?" —*James Hermoe St. James, Minnesota*

Pride and Prayer

WHILE hiking through the wilds of Africa, a missionary walked right into a pride of lions. They roared and started to chase him.

The missionary ran as fast as he could, but every time he looked over his shoulder the lions were gaining on him. He knew he had only a matter of seconds, so he dropped to his knees and prayed.

After a few minutes, he stopped and listened. All was quiet. He turned and saw the lions on the ground behind him, their eyes closed.

"I didn't know lions prayed," he said in amazement.

One of the lions replied, "*You're* praying. We're saying grace." —*Steve Smith Eaton, Ohio*

Just One Question

GOD CAME to a woman in church and told her, "I will answer any question you ask me, but only one, so make it a good one."

The woman asked, "How old will I live to be?"

"One hundred and nine," God replied.

The woman decided if she was going to live that long, she'd better take care of herself. She had a tummy tuck, some liposuction, a face-lift and a nose job. Then she got run over by a bus.

When the woman got to Heaven, she told God, "I thought I was going to live to 109!"

"I'm sorry," God said. "I didn't recognize you."
—*Myrl Hawley Onondaga, Michigan*

Fools Rush In

THE FAMOUS NAVY chaplain, Father Joe Callahan, was serving at the Naval Air Station in Pensacola, Florida when a sailor approached. "Chaplain, is that the straight stuff about Christ walking on water?" the sailor asked.

"Yes, it is," Father Joe said.

"You said that anyone who had enough faith could do it, too," the sailor continued.

"That's right," the chaplain said.

"Then why don't you walk out on the bay right now?"

"Well, son, I'm afraid some darned fool like you might try to follow me."

Remedial Study Required

WHILE visiting the second-grade Sunday school class, the pastor asked the children if they knew what happened on Easter.

One lad raised his hand and said, "George Washington crossed a river and blew up firecrackers." The teacher blushed in embarrassment.

Suddenly another boy's hand shot up. "I know what happened on Easter Sunday," he said. "Jesus rose from the dead!"

The teacher and pastor were elated—until the boy went on, "And when He didn't see His shadow, He went back in again."—*Bob Brand Cannon Falls, Minnesota*

The Great Flood

A FRIEND of ours, a retired minister, keeps copies of all his old sermons in the basement. During a recent flood, his wife went downstairs to check for water. "Did my sermons get wet?" he called down. "No," she called back, "they're just as dry as ever."

—Gene Blumenschein Milford Center, Ohio

Excuses, Excuses

ANDY MISSED Mass more often than not. Father Murphy met him on the street one day and asked why he didn't come to church more regularly.

"There are too many hypocrites in church," Andy replied.

"Well," the priest said, "there's always room for one more."

Who's Afraid?

AN OLD FARMER went to church one Sunday and took a seat near the front. Halfway through the sermon, the preacher ran out of the church in terror, followed by the entire congregation—except the farmer.

The Devil walked up to the farmer and said, "Why didn't you leave with the rest of them? Don't you know who I am?"

"Yes, you're the Devil," the farmer said.

"So why didn't you run out, too?" the Devil persisted. "Aren't you even afraid of me?"

"No," the farmer said. "I lived with your sister for 50 years." *—Lee Chamberlain Dexter, Missouri*

For Whom the Bell Tolls

A CATHOLIC university advertised for a bell-ringer. The first applicant was a man with no arms. "You can't possibly do the job," the priest told him. The man insisted he could.

The priest took him to the bell tower, where the man made the most beautiful music ever heard, by ringing the bell with his face. Unfortunately, he fell from the tower and was killed. When someone asked who the man was, the priest said, "I don't know, but his face sure rings a bell."

The next day, the dead man's brother came and asked for the job. The priest took him to the bell tower, but he, too, fell and was killed. Asked who the man was, the priest said, "I don't know, but he's a dead ringer

"There's Methuselah — whatever you do,
don't ask him about the old days."

for his brother."
—*Jim O'Hara*
Morris, Illinois

Checked and Double-Checked

A RICH CONTRACTOR was dying. His wife asked the parish priest to visit and put him in a spiritual frame of mind. The priest suggested the man donate $10,000 to the church for a stained-glass window, with any inscription he liked.

Just then the doctor came in and gave the man a bill for $50,000. The dying man wrote a check to the doctor, then one to the priest. "And what would you like inscribed on the window?" the priest asked.

The man replied, "In honor of Patrick J. Murphy, who died like Christ—between two thieves." —*Rita Witges*
Scheller, Illinois

Going Up?

"HOW MANY of you would like to go to Heaven?" the Sunday school teacher asked. All the children raised a hand except for one little boy.

Surprised, the teacher asked him why he didn't want to go to Heaven.

"I'm sorry," the boy said. "Mommy told me to come right home after Sunday school." —*Lucille Stamper*
Danville, Indiana

Man of Few Words

AFTER the death of his father, Ed met with the minister to plan the service. "Did your father have any words of wisdom I could share with the mourners at the funeral?" the minister asked. "No," Ed replied, "Mom was with him to the very end."
—*Marlene Webb*
Ewing, Illinois

It's a Puzzle

AFTER CHURCH one Sunday, John told his friend, Fred, he'd noticed that teenagers weren't mentioned in the Bible. "God speaks about adults and children, but never teenagers," he said.

Fred replied, "God's just like everybody else. He didn't know what to do with teenagers, either."
—*Fred Buttke*
North Hudson, Wisconsin

Nearer, My God, To Thee

TWO WOMEN spent much of an afternoon trying to impress each other with how religious they were. When one woman left to go home, the other turned to her husband, who'd been quietly smoking his pipe.

"You know," she said, "Mrs. Brown is a good Christian, but I believe I live closer to the Lord."

Her husband puffed for a moment, then observed, "Ain't either of you crowding Him any."

ing by falling asleep as soon as the sermon began. Finally she asked the pastor what to do. "I think I can help," he said. "When you come to church next Sunday, wrap a piece of Limburger cheese in a handkerchief and put it in your purse."

Next Sunday, Mr. Jones fell asleep as soon as the pastor began preaching. Mrs. Jones removed the cheese from her purse and waved it under his nose. Her husband stirred and muttered just loud enough for all to hear, "Maggie, you've got your feet on the pillow again." —*Charles Porter Terre Haute, Indiana*

Good Morning To You

THE MINISTER was waiting when his teenage daughter returned home from a dance at 3 a.m.

"Good morning, child of the Devil," he thundered.

The girl answered respectfully, "Good morning, Father."

A Fragrant Foul

MR. JONES embarrassed his wife every Sunday morn-

Forget About It

A SERIOUSLY ILL MAN called his pastor to his sickbed. "Pastor," he said, "If you pray for me to recover and I do, I'll give you $25,000 toward the new church you're building."

The pastor prayed, and the man got well. But the man never made good on his pledge. The pastor hinted at it several times with no success. Finally he reminded the man bluntly, "You promised to give $25,000 for the new church if you got well."

"Did I?" the man exclaimed. "Well, that should give you some idea how sick I was."

Everything Old Is New Again

A MINISTER was called out of town unexpectedly and asked his assistant to fill in for him on Sunday. When the minister came home, he asked his wife what she'd thought of the assistant's sermon.

"Poorest sermon I've ever heard," she said. "There was nothing in it at all. It didn't even make sense."

Later that day, the minister asked his assistant how things had gone.

"Fine, sir, absolutely wonderful," the young man replied. "I didn't have time to prepare anything myself, so I preached one of your old sermons."

Burning Questions, Smoldering Answers

HERE ARE some children's responses to questions about various Bible teachings.

• Noah's wife was called Joan of Ark.

• The epistles were the wives of the apostles.

• The fourth commandment is "Humor thy father and mother".

• Eskimos are God's frozen people.

• The Tower of Babel is where Solomon kept his wives.

• Holy acrimony is another name for marriage.

• The eighth commandment is "Thou shalt not witness thy bare neighbor".

• Christians have one wife. They call it monotony.

A Fuelish Fable

AS a goodwill gesture, the owner of a small-town service station offered free fill-ups to ministers. The word spread, and before long he was pumping gas for every clergyman in the county. But his generosity got the best of him, and soon the station was closed.

As the sheriff was carting away the last of the equipment, a passerby wondered why the station had gone out of business.

"Well," the sheriff drawled, "you can fuel some of the parsons some of the time, but you can't fuel all of the parsons all of the time."

That's Teamwork

WHILE taking a walk in the country, Parson Green paused to rest against Farmer Harper's fence. He knew the family had saved a long time to buy this farm, which had needed lots of work.

When he saw the farmer, he walked over to him and said, "Joel, you and the Lord have done a mighty fine piece of work on this property."

The exhausted farmer turned slowly and said, "Meaning no disrespect, Parson, but did you *see* this place when the Lord had it to himself?"

—*Barb Hanselman*
Angola, Indiana

Let There Be Light

THE MINISTER of a small country church wanted to make some much-needed improvements and suggested buying a chandelier. The parishioners voted it down.

"Why do you oppose buying a chandelier?" the pastor asked.

"First, no one can spell it," a spokesman explained.

"Second, no one can play it. And third, what we really need is more light."

Help Wanted, Proofreader

THE FOLLOWING ITEMS appeared in church bulletins:

• Barbara C. remains in the hospital and needs blood donors for more transfusions. She is also having trouble sleeping and requests tapes of Brother Jack's sermons.

• The used clothing sale will begin at 1 p.m. If things don't sell, there will be a price reduction later in the day. Ladies' skirts would drop at 4 p.m., and men's pants lowered shortly after.

• The Over 60's Choir will be disbanded for the summer with the thanks of the entire church.

• The church women are planning an English Tea Party, inviting the women of area Lutheran churches. All women are asked to wear hats and gloves; no slacks please.

• Midweek services are still focusing on the Seven Deadly Sins. This week, "Greed and Gluttony". Join us for services at 7:30, and come earlier for soup and salad at 6:30.

• Come and celebrate! Pastor Steve will present his last sermon on Sunday.

• Remember in prayer the many who are sick of our community.

• Weight Watchers will meet at 7 p.m. at the First Presbyterian Church. Please use the large double door at the side entrance.

The Power of Prayer

A PREACHER died and found himself behind a New York cab driver in line at the Pearly Gates.

St. Peter told the cabbie his reward would be a mansion with a swimming pool and a limousine.

Then St. Peter turned to the preacher and said, "Welcome. Your heavenly reward is a beautiful oak walking stick."

"Wait a minute," the preacher protested. "I preached God's word for over 60 years. Why does the cab driver get so much, when I only get a walking stick?"

St. Peter smiled and said, "When you preached, people slept. When the cabbie

drove, people prayed."
—*Roger Kays*
La Habra, California

Postage Due

A WOMAN went to the post office to buy stamps to mail her daughter's wedding invitations.

"I'd like 200 stamps, please," she told the clerk.

"What denomination?" the clerk asked.

"Oh, dear," the woman said. "I suppose it would be best to split them. Give me 100 Baptist and 100 Presbyterian." —*Bob Gaskill*
Neligh, Nebraska

Long-Lasting Message

AT THE END of a church service, a woman thanked the pastor for his sermon. "I found it so helpful," she said.

The minister said, "I hope it won't be as helpful as the last sermon you heard me preach."

At that, the perplexed woman asked, "What do you mean?"

"Well," the clergyman explained, "that sermon lasted you 3 months."

"Excuse me, but wouldn't these be a lot lighter on floppy disks?"

You *Can* Get There From Here

AT A SPECIAL Mass for preschoolers, the priest talked to the children about being good and going to Heaven. At the end of his sermon, he asked the youngsters, "Where do you want to go?"

"Heaven!" they shouted.

Then the priest asked, "And what must you be to get to Heaven?"

Without hesitation, a chorus of little voices yelled, "Dead!"

The Blind Shall See

ONE SUMMER DAY, several nuns were working on a

remodeling project in the church. The heat was unbearable. "You know," one nun said, "if we locked the doors and shut the stained-glass windows, we could work in our underwear." So they did.

About an hour later, there was a knock on the door. The startled nuns called out, "Who is it?"

"It's the blind man," came the reply.

One nun said, "Let him in—he can't see anything."

The man walked into the foyer and said, "Nice undies. Now, where do you want these blinds?"

Does This Ring A Bell?

A MINISTER was walking along a residential street lined with fine old Victorian homes. It was bitterly cold and overcast, and the lawns were covered with snow.

Suddenly he spotted a small boy on a front porch, trying to ring an old-fashioned manual doorbell. The bell was set high in the door, and the boy was jumping in a vain attempt to reach it. Every now and then the boy paused to warm his hands

by rubbing and blowing on them.

Poor little tike, the minister thought. He walked over to the porch, patted the boy on the shoulder and rang the bell vigorously. "And now what, my little man?" the minister said, smiling down at him.

"Now," the boy said breathlessly, "we run like crazy!"

In the Spirit

WHEN a new preacher came to a country church, some of the members heard he liked an occasional nip of wine.

To find out if this rumor was true, two members visited him and presented him with a bottle of "spirits".

They said it was a gift from the congregation and insisted he thank them in his sermon on Sunday. The preacher hesitated, but finally agreed.

The next Sunday, the preacher told the congregation, "I was recently very favorably impressed with the generous gift of fruit from the congregation. But most of all, I appreciate the spirit in which it was given."

—Ira Frost, Marion, Ohio

Took Her Pick

A WOMAN had been a faithful church worker for years. At an evening service, the pastor thanked her for her contributions and said, "We shall reward her by letting her pick three hymns for the evening."

The woman rose and said, "How wonderful!" Then she pointed to various members of the congregation and said, "I'll take him and him and him."
—*Rea Kenyon, Guthrie, Iowa*

Confessing Their Sins

FOUR MINISTERS were riding home together after a conference on the importance of confession in the modern church.

Their casual talk turned serious as they started putting what they'd learned into practice and confessing to each other.

"I must confess," the first minister said, "that my great sin is greed. I really enjoy funerals because I know I'll be paid for them."

The second minister said, "My sin is gambling. I really enjoy taking chances. I'm not such a big ecumenical man—I just enjoy the Catholics' bingo games."

"My big sin is women," said the third. "I enjoy looking at beautiful women. I'd even have to call it lust."

The three clergymen continued to share more details of their sins, until they noticed the fourth minister hadn't said a word.

"What about you, Harry?" they asked. "What's your big sin?"

"Well," Harry replied, "my sin is repeating gossip to others—and I can't wait to get home!"

Praying for Mercy

TWO MEN went to the front of the church to pray. One was a leading citizen in the community and the other a schoolteacher.

The prominent citizen turned his eyes upward and said, "Oh Lord, I thank Thee that I am not like these professional men, even as this poor schoolmaster. I subscribe liberally to foreign missions and to all the work of the church. It is my money that advances your cause."

The prayer said by the schoolteacher was quite different. He humbly bowed his head and said, "Oh God, be merciful to me. I was that man's teacher."

Old But Useful

FROM a church bulletin: "Rummage sale Sunday, church basement. Ladies, now's your chance to get rid of your old but still useful items. Bring your husbands." —*Louise Eppers Fort Madison, Iowa*

Choice Words

THE GOLF PRO invited a priest to the course to play a round. But when they finished, the pro handed him a bill for $20, much to the priest's dismay.

The priest wanted to tell the pro what he thought of him without using offensive language. As he handed over the $20, he told the pro, "Tell your father and mother to come over sometime, and I'll marry them."

Wake-Up Call

SUNDAY SERVICES at one church were usually followed by a breakfast of coffee and rolls. The pastor asked a little boy why he thought this was done. The child answered, "I guess it's to wake people up after the sermon so they can drive home."

Men at Work

A PRIEST was called to attend to a parishioner who'd had a heart attack, but couldn't find a parking space. He pulled into a no-parking zone and left a note on the windshield that read, "Priest at work inside".

When he returned to his car, he found a ticket, with a note that read, "Policeman at work outside".

Fishing For an Answer

A SUNDAY School teacher asked her young class how Noah spent his time on the ark. After a minute with no answers, she prompted, "Do you suppose he did a lot of fishing?"

"Probably not," piped up one lad. "He only had two worms." —*Weldon Warren Mesquite, Texas*

Sink or Swim

A RABBI, a Christian and a Buddhist were sitting in a boat on a lake. The rabbi said, "Because I have faith in God, I can walk on water." He stepped out of the boat and walked to shore.

The Christian said, "Because *I* have faith in God, *I* can walk on water." He, too, stepped out and walked to shore.

The Buddhist looked at the water, then at his friends, and said, "If they can do it, so can I." He stepped out of the boat and tumbled into the water.

The rabbi turned to the Christian and said, "Do you think we should have told him where the stepping stones were?"
—*Rhonda Barfknecht
Elmore, Minnesota*

Silence is Golden

A MAN became a monk and took a vow of silence. After 5 years, he was allowed to speak two words. "Hard bed," he said.

After another 5 years of silence, the monk was allowed to say two more words. "Bad food," he said.

For another 5 years, the monk said nothing. Then he was allowed to speak two more words. "Want out," he said.

"You might as well leave," the head of the monastery said. "You've been complaining ever since you got here."
—*Marge Wisslead
Colchester, Illinois*

A Good Investment

A CONVENT was willed a small estate, with $50 going to each nun to give away as she saw fit.

Sister Catherine Ann decided to give her $50 to the first poor person she saw. Just then she looked out the window and saw a sad-looking man leaning against a telephone pole across the street.

She immediately went to him, convinced he'd been sent by God to receive her gift. She pressed the $50 into the man's hand, saying, "Godspeed, my good man." As she turned to leave, the man asked her name. "Sister Catherine Ann," she replied shyly.

The following evening, the man came to the convent, rang the bell and asked for Sister Catherine Ann. "I'm afraid I can't disturb her now," another nun said. "She's in the chapel. May I give her a message?"

"You can," the visitor grinned. "Give her this hundred bucks and tell her 'Godspeed' came in second."
—*Tom Keegan*
Wamego, Kansas

Ministry or Menagerie?

A LADY who fancied herself a social climber was seated next to the local priest at a charity affair and decided to put the pastor in his place.

"*Our* minister," she stated coldly, "is an Eagle, an Elk, a Moose and a Lion."

"Indeed," the priest mused. "How much does it cost to see him?"

Chapter and Verse

A MINISTER told his congregation he would preach a sermon on lying the following Sunday and asked them to read the 17th chapter of Mark.

The next Sunday, he asked how many had done the reading he'd requested. Several hands went up.

"I see," the minister said.

"You are the very people I want to reach. Mark only has 16 chapters."

Alms for the Poor

A FATHER and his young son were in church. Just before the collection plate was passed, the father gave the son a quarter to put in the plate.

When the plate was passed, the boy palmed the quarter. After the service, the boy approached the preacher and said, "I want to give you this quarter."

"That's very kind of you, son," the preacher said, "but you could have put it in the collection plate."

"No, Preacher, I want to give it to you personally, because my father says you're the poorest preacher in town." —*Warren Worcester*
Southwest Harbor, Maine

Words of Wizzzdom

AFTER SERVICES, a minister asked a member of the congregation, "Did you get anything out of my sermon?"

"Yes," the man replied. "A nap."

Once is Enough

A YOUNG WOMAN confessed to the priest that she'd allowed her sweetheart to kiss her. "How many times did you allow him to do so?" the priest asked.

"I'm just confessing," the woman replied. "I'm not here to brag."

"How long ago did this happen?" the priest asked.

"Ten years ago, and I've confessed it several times."

"You only have to confess it once," the priest said.

"I know, Father. But it's a pleasant memory, and I like to talk about it."

One More Time

ON A COLD January day in Tennessee, a man was being baptized in a river. The preacher asked him, "Is the water cold?"

"Naw," the convert said.

One of the deacons shouted, "Dip him again, Preacher—he's still lyin'."

Deeply Mistaken

A DOCTOR and a priest were driving past a cemetery. The priest said, "You know, Doc, a lot of your mistakes are buried there."

"That's true," the doctor said. "The only difference between us is that your mistakes are buried a little deeper." —*Tom Keegan Wamego, Kansas*

Pastoral Care

PRESIDENT Woodrow Wilson's father was a minister. One day the pastor was driving his fine horse down the street when a member of his congregation spotted him.

"Pastor, your horse looks better than you do," the parishioner said.

Mr. Wilson replied, "Yes, I take care of my horse. My congregation looks after me."

That's a Plateful

A BANKER'S SON bragged to his pals, "My father makes $85 an hour just sitting at a desk."

"So?" answered the lawyer's son. "My father talks for an hour and makes $150."

"That's nothing," said the minister's child. "My father preaches for an hour and it takes four men to collect the money." —*Susan Fulton Waynesboro, Georgia*

Something to Crow About

A KANSAS farm family invited the outgoing and incoming pastors of their church to Sunday dinner. The farmer's wife fried two chickens, which the clergymen polished off in short order.

After the meal, the farmer was showing his guests around the barnyard when an old rooster let out a magnificent crow. "He seems mighty proud of himself," one of the ministers observed.

"He should," muttered the farmer. "He's got two sons in the ministry."

Sounds About Right

A LITTLE BOY came running home from his first Sunday school class. His father asked, "Well, son, what did you learn?"

"I learned about a cross-eyed bear named Gladly," the boy said.

"That's something new,"
his father said. "Tell me about it."

"We sang a song about him," said the boy. "It was called *Gladly the Cross I'd Bear.*"
—*Emerson Vandenhouten Luxemburg, Wisconsin*

Handle With Care

A DEVOUT WOMAN carefully wrapped a Bible and took it to the post office to mail to her son in the military.

"Say, lady," the clerk inquired, "does this package contain anything breakable?"

The woman replied quickly, "Only the Ten Commandments".

Homework Can Wait

A COUNTRY PASTOR was preaching about Judgment Day.

"Thunder will roar, flames will shoot out from the heavens...floods, storms and earthquakes will devastate the world!" he intoned.

Wide-eyed, a little farm boy turned to his mother and whispered, "Will I get to skip school that day?"

Now That's Important

THE POPE flew to New York City and had several hours before his first meeting, so he asked the limousine driver to show him the sights.

After a couple of hours, the driver said there wasn't much more to see. Was there anything else His Holiness would like to do?

"I've always wanted to drive a limousine," the Pope said. "Would that be all right?" The driver assured him it would and climbed in back.

The Pope promptly ran a red light and was stopped by a policeman. The officer asked for his driver's license, then said, "Just a minute. I have to call the station."

The officer radioed his sergeant and said, "I stopped a VIP and need a little advice."

"Is it a councilman or the mayor?" the sergeant asked.

"No, this guy's bigger than that."

"Oh, you stopped a senator?"

"No, he's bigger than that."

"Don't tell me you stopped the President!" the sergeant said.

"No, he's bigger than that."

"There's no one bigger than the President of the United States!" the sergeant yelled. "Who did you stop?"

"I don't know," the policeman replied, "but the Pope is driving him around."

—*Donna Binkley*
Bluffton, Indiana

Hush, Little Baby

DURING the minister's sermon, a boy began crying near the front of the church. Unable to quiet him, his mother got up to take him out.

The minister stopped and said, "Don't take him out. He's not bothering me."

The woman turned and said, "No, but you're sure bothering him."

—*Joanne Latham*
Kenton, Ohio

Be Quiet Up There

A FAITHFUL Catholic woman was pouring her heart out before the statue of the Blessed Mother at her parish church. Thinking she was alone, she prayed aloud, asking for a number of personal favors.

"Why do we get all dressed up for church when the minister wears a nightgown?"

She didn't know it, but a worker was touching up a painting on the wall behind the high altar. The painter decided to have some fun and called out in a somber tone, "This is Jesus. We are busy right now. Please come back another time."

Though momentarily shocked, the woman quickly regained her composure and snapped, "Quiet. I'm talking to your Mother."

Kegling Clergy

DID YOU HEAR the one about the ministers who formed a bowling team? They called themselves the Holy Rollers. —*Christy Blue Lincoln, Nebraska*

Pastor William?

WHILE Mom and Dad prepared the table, their young son told the preacher they were having goat for dinner. The boy's father overheard him and laughed. "No, son, we're not having goat," he chuckled.

"Yes, we are," the boy insisted. "I heard you tell Mom we were having the old goat for dinner on Sunday."
—Sheila Lang
Walnut Grove, Mississippi

Have We Met?

CHARLIE took an active part in just about everything going on in town—except church. Try as his wife might, she just couldn't talk him into attending services.

One Sunday, she broke down his resistance and even persuaded him to greet churchgoers at the door. Charlie hailed almost everyone by name, until the church was filled and services were about to begin.

At the last minute, a straggler appeared. Charlie shook his hand, said he was glad to see him and expressed the hope he'd be back the following Sunday.

"Oh, I'll be back," the latecomer said cheerfully, then walked down the aisle and up into the pulpit.

A Hot Time

AFTER A PREACHER died, a neighbor with the same name went to California on business.

The businessman sent his wife a telegram, which was delivered to the preacher's wife by mistake. The message read, "Arrived safe—heat terrific!"

Now That's Living

OVER COFFEE at the local cafe, a preacher, a priest and a rabbi were discussing the question of when life begins.

"Life begins at conception," the priest said.

"No," countered the rabbi. "I believe life begins at birth."

The preacher sipped his coffee as he pondered the question. Finally he said, "You're both wrong. Life begins when the last child leaves home and the dog dies."
—Corwin Goodman
Lime Springs, Iowa

Hold That Thought

TWO MEN had been shipwrecked and were floating on a raft. One began to pray, "Oh Lord, I've broken most of the Commandments. I've been an awful sinner all my days. Lord, if you'll just spare me, I'll..."

"Hold on—don't commit yourself," the other shouted. "I think I see a sail."

That's My Boy!

FOUR shamefully proud mothers each had a son in the ministry. One mother boasted, "When my son walks into the room, everyone stands and says, 'Good morning, Bishop'."

Not to be outdone, the second mother said, "When my son walks into the room, everyone stands and says, 'Good morning, Archbishop'."

"When my son walks into a room, everyone kneels and says, 'Good morning, Your Eminence'," bragged the third mother.

The fourth mother's son was an ex-farm boy humbly serving a poor rural congregation. But she said, "My son stands 6-foot-7 and weighs 375 pounds. When he walks into the room, everyone looks up and says, 'Oh, my Lord'!"

—*Wayne Becker*
Blairstown, Iowa

Called His Bluff

A PRIEST and a rabbi, who had become the best of friends, were having dinner together.

"Come on," said the priest to the rabbi. "When are you going to let yourself go and enjoy a piece of ham?"

"At your wedding," the rabbi replied.

Now, Don't Cause A Scene

WHEN my sister found her two young sons arguing in the living room, she scolded them. "Don't you know God is right here watching you argue?" she said.

"Then let's go in the bedroom and finish," the older boy suggested.

—*J. Hampsch*
Los Angeles, California

Pleasant Dreams

IF all the people who sleep in church were laid end to end... they'd be more comfortable. —*Kenneth Dooley*
Marion, Indiana

Weighty Question

TWO BROTHERS ran a coal business in a small town. During a revival, one of the brothers was converted to Christianity. For weeks, he tried to persuade his partner to do the same.

"Why can't you become a Christian and join the church like I did?" he finally asked.

"It's a fine thing for *you* to belong to the church," his brother said. "But if I join, who'll weigh the coal?"

Stop-and-Go Traffic

A PREACHER had a horse for sale, and a cowboy came to buy it. After they agreed on a price, the preacher explained that the horse had become very religious in their years together.

"To get the horse to go, all you have to do is say 'Praise the Lord'," the preacher explained. "To get him to stop, just say 'Amen'."

The cowboy jumped into the saddle to ride home and yelled, "Praise the Lord"! The horse immediately took off at a gallop. Faster and faster he went—straight toward a cliff.

The cowboy couldn't remember how to get the horse to stop. "Whoa! Whoa!" he hollered. But the horse wouldn't stop.

The horse and cowboy were about ready to go over the cliff. The cowboy figured he was going to meet his Maker, so he bowed his head and whispered, "Amen".

At that, the horse skidded to a stop 2 feet from the edge of the cliff. The cowboy looked over the edge to the jagged rocks below. Overcome with joy that his life had been spared, he yelled, "Praise the Lord"!
—*Aden Yoder*
Greenwich, Ohio

Great Sales Pitch

A CATHOLIC GIRL began dating a Baptist boy. As the relationship grew more serious, the worried girl told her mother, "I can't marry him. He's a Baptist, you know."

"Then sell him on Catholicism," her mother said. "He'll never be in a better mood to buy."

Some time later, the girl came home weeping.

"What's the matter?" her mother asked.

"I oversold him," the girl cried. "Now he's going to be a priest!"

Come On In

A MINISTER went to call on a family who attended his church. The family had just bought a big mean-looking dog, and it was standing in the yard, growling. The minister stopped outside the gate.

The lady of the house came to the door and called, "Come on in."

"Will the dog bite?" the preacher asked.

"I don't know," the woman said. "That's what we want to find out."

Paul's Pen Pals?

THE SERMON was on the apostle Paul and his epistles, and when the service had ended, one lad approached the minister.

"I was wondering," the boy said. "Did the Corinthians ever write back?"

On Shank's Mare

A HIGH-SCHOOL senior went to his dad in January and said he wanted a new car for graduation.

His father said, "I'll get you that new car, but first you must do three things— bring your grades up, read the Bible more and get a haircut."

In May, the son went to his father and asked, "How am I doing? Am I going to get a new car for graduation?"

"Son, you've brought your average up from a 'C' to an 'A'. That's great," the father said. "I've also noticed that you've been studying the Scriptures every morning before school. That's wonderful. But you still haven't had a haircut."

"But, Dad," the son protested, "while studying the Bible, I've noticed that Moses and Jesus are always depicted in the illustrations as having long hair."

The father replied, "Son, you must remember that Moses and Jesus walked everywhere they went. And so will you." —*Jack Mackin St. Anthony, Iowa*

"Reverend Smith always seems to know where to catch the big ones."

Anybody Up There?

A MAN traveling alone had stopped at a scenic mountain overlook to take some pictures. He ventured too close to the edge of the precipice and fell into the abyss. Just before he reached the bottom, he grabbed a small tree growing out of a crevasse. Hanging on for dear life, he began to call for help.

"Is anybody up there?" he

called again and again.

After several hours, his cry was answered. "Yes," a deep voice said. "I am here. Can I help you?"

"You sure can," the man called. "Get a rope and rescue me."

"If you have faith, I can save you," the voice replied. "Do you have faith?"

"Yes, I've got faith," the man yelled, "but hurry up before I fall!"

"If you have faith," the voice said, "do as I say, and you'll be all right. Just let go of that tree."

After a few moments of silence, the man cried out, "Is there anybody else up there?"

Sorry to Bother You

AN OLD-TIME circuit rider was walking in his yard, which was surrounded by a high fence.

A roughneck who'd been offended by the man's preaching rode his horse into the enclosure, climbed down and said, "Parson, you've got to lick me or get out of this neck of the woods."

The preacher quietly took him by the nape of the neck and the seat of his pants and deposited him over the fence. The ruffian got up, peeked through a crack in the fence and said meekly, "Now, Parson, if you'll hand my mare over the fence, too, I'll be a-goin'."

A Cents-ible Response

A MAN was trying to understand the nature of God, and asked Him a few questions.

"God, how long is a million years to you?"

God said, "A million years is like a minute."

Then the man asked, "God, how much is a million dollars to you?"

God said, "A million dollars is like a penny."

The man thought about this, then asked, "God, will you give me a penny?"

God replied, "In a minute."
—*John and Irene Krueger*
Cresco, Iowa

Tight Budget

A YOUNG MAN asked his preacher, "Can I live a good Christian life on $30 a week?"

The preacher replied dryly, "That's all you can do."

Full of Hot Air

A MINISTER thought it was a good idea when his church replaced paper towels in the rest rooms with hot-air dryers. He changed his mind after he saw a sign over the machine that read, "For a sermon from our fine preacher, just press the button."

A Heavenly Chorus

FROM a church bulletin: "Tonight's sermon: 'What is hell?' Come early and listen to our choir practice."

—Ken Anderson
Monmouth, Illinois

Stroke of Genius

A PASTOR had been trying in vain to find time to golf. In desperation, he called in sick one Sunday morning and sneaked out to the golf course.

Two angels were watching as he teed up on the first hole. He teed off, and one of the angels swooped down, caught the ball in midair, and dropped it into the cup.

"You gave that slacker a hole-in-one!" the other angel cried. "Why on earth would you do that?"

The first angel just smiled serenely and said, "Who can he tell?"

—Edna Rassler
Albert City, Iowa

Doing It the Hard Way

THE OLD PARSON was one of the world's worst golfers. He decided to improve his game and began practicing at every opportunity.

One day he was playing—badly, as usual—and hit a typical tee shot on a par-3 hole. The ball flew to the woods at the left, ricocheted off a tree across the fairway and bounced off another tree in the direction of the green.

As the ball approached the green, it struck a stone and gained enough momentum to reach the cup and drop in. It was a hole-in-one.

The astonished clergyman turned his eyes Heavenward and begged, "Please, Father, I'd rather do it myself."

The Book Was Better

AFTER THE MOVIE *The*

Bible was completed, a rumor circulated that there would be a top-secret screening for the studio brass. As the other staff members whispered about the event, each warned the next to keep it quiet.

One worker was bewildered. "Why is this such a big secret?" she asked.

"I'm not sure," her co-worker said. "Maybe they don't want anyone to give away the plot."

That's No Lady, That's My Wife

A LUTHERAN PASTOR in clerical garb was speeding down the highway with his wife beside him. An Irish patrolman pulled him over and began reading him the riot act.

Then the officer noticed what the driver was wearing. Mistaking the man for a Catholic priest, the officer gave him a polite warning and sent him on his way.

As they drove off, the woman told her husband, "It wasn't nice of you to let that patrolman think you were a priest."

"Don't worry about who he thought *I* was," her husband replied. "You should be more concerned about who he thought *you* were."
—*Levi Snyder*
Adams, Wisconsin

Toll Charges Apply

A MINISTER placed a long-distance call. "I'd like to speak to the Reverend Miller Palmer," he said. "This is Reverend Baxter."

"Is this a station-to-station call?" the operator asked.

"No," the minister said. "This is a parson-to-parson call."
—*John Hoyt*
Galena, Ohio

Life-and-Death Questions

RICHARD Cardinal Cushing told about the time he was called to give last rites to a man at the scene of an accident.

"Do you believe in God the Father, God the Son and God the Holy Ghost?" he asked.

The man replied, "Father, here I am dying, and you bother me with riddles."

Take Me Out To the Ballgame

BILL was a big baseball fan. One day he asked his minister, "Is there baseball in Heaven? I have to know!"

The reverend fasted and prayed for divine revelation, and his prayer was answered. He went to Bill and said, "I have good news and bad news.

"First, the good news. Yes, there *is* baseball in Heaven," the minister said.

"So what's the bad news?" Bill asked.

"You're pitching tomorrow."
—*Daniel Sheaffer*
Jeromesville, Ohio

Tempting Fate

A PRIEST drove to town and parked in a no-parking zone. He slipped this note under the windshield wiper: "I have circled this block 10 times, but couldn't find a parking spot. I have an appointment to keep. Forgive us our trespasses."

When he returned to his car, he found a parking ticket, with this note attached: "I have circled this block for 10 years. If I don't give you a ticket, I lose my job. Lead us not into temptation."
—*Randy Seys*
Mankato, Minnesota

In the Proper Denomination

A DISTRAUGHT FARMER knocked on the local priest's door. Tears were rolling down the farmer's face as he cradled his just-deceased pet dog in his arms.

"Father," the farmer sniffled, "could you please preside over a service for ol' 'Ruff'? Maybe say a few words to send him off proper? It sure would mean a lot to me."

"Well, son," the priest said gently, "I know your pet was a dear friend, and my heart aches at your grief. But I'm afraid we just can't hold a service for a dog in our church. I hope you understand."

As the disappointed farmer turned to leave, the priest added, "Perhaps the church down the road would be able to help you."

At that, the farmer brightened a bit and asked, "Do you think $25,000 would be enough to offer them for the service?"

"Just a moment, my son,"

the priest said. "You didn't tell me the dog was Catholic."

—Troy Hildebrandt
Waukesha, Wisconsin

Cashing It In

WHILE READING his morning paper, a man exclaimed to his wife, "Listen to this! The cashier at the bank has absconded with $60,000. What's more, he stole one of the executive's limousines and ran off with the bank president's wife."

"Why, that's awful," his wife said. "Who will teach his Sunday school class next week?"

Move On Back

THE BUS DRIVER for a parochial school was urging his young passengers to move to the rear of the bus, with little success.

Finally, in desperation, he shouted, "Fill up the back—just like you do in church!"

Gardening Tips

A PRIEST illustrated a point in his sermon by saying that a wise God knows who grows best in sunlight and who needs the protection of shade.

"You know that you plant roses in the sun," he explained, "but if you want your fuchsias to grow they must be in a shady nook."

After Mass, a woman sought him out. "Father, you don't know how much your sermon has helped me," she enthused.

The priest was thrilled, but then the woman added, "Until today, I never realized what was wrong with my fuchsias."

It Makes Sense

DURING a bad dry spell, our parish priest scheduled a Thursday Mass and asked everyone to come and pray for rain.

Two bachelor brothers farmed nearby, but didn't come to church much, so the priest dropped by and asked them to attend.

The oldest brother came to the service...alone. After Mass, the priest approached him and said, "Good to see you in church to pray for rain, Ben. But where's your brother, Hubert?"

Ben quickly answered, "He had to stay home to close the windows."

—Mickey Sowada
St. Joseph, Minnesota

Somnambulistic Sermon

ONE SUNDAY a man got up right in the middle of the preacher's sermon and walked out. After church, his embarrassed wife sought out the preacher to explain. "I hope you don't think he disagreed with what you said," she told him. "He just has a tendency to walk in his sleep." —*Kenneth Dooley Marion, Indiana*

A Small Don't-ation

AS the offering plate was being passed down the aisle toward him, a little boy piped up just loud enough for the whole congregation to hear, "Don't pay for me, Daddy. Kids under 5 are free!"

A Self-Made Man

THE WEALTHIEST MAN in town seldom went to church, and when he did, he never put anything in the collection plate. On one such Sunday, the pastor spoke to him coldly after services.

"Look, Preacher," the man said, "I know you disapprove of me. But I don't part with my money easily. I made every cent I have the hard way. You see, I'm a self-made man."

"Well, sir," the pastor countered, "that relieves the Almighty of a great responsibility."

Let the Buyer Beware

DEACON SMITH was the sharpest horse trader in the hollow and the most noted Bible scholar. No matter how questionable the transaction, he could always cite a verse of Scripture that would apply.

When a city fellow moved to the hollow, the deacon persuaded him to pay top dollar for his oldest horse, a swaybacked, spavined creature. Deacon Smith's wife was outraged.

"Well, you ought to be ashamed of yourself, getting that poor ignorant city feller to buy that broken-down nag! Now, tell me, what Bible verse can you come up with to justify that?"

The deacon thought a

"Read him last Sunday's sermon. *That* will put him to sleep."

minute, then said, "He was a stranger, and I took him in."

—*Alice Hemminger*
Oak Harbor, Ohio

Plenty to Choose

A PREACHER asked an emergency medical technician about the most unusual 911 call he'd ever had.

"It was at a church," the EMT replied. "The usher had noticed an elderly gentleman slumped over. On checking, he found the man was dead, so he called 911. We carried out four men before we got the right one."

—*Marilyn Seibert*
Spencerville, Ohio

He Said a Mouthful

THE PEWS were packed for the new pastor's first service, but he preached for only 5 minutes. The parishioners thought the sermon was excellent, though a little short.

The next Sunday, the pastor again preached for just 5 minutes. The elders discussed this, but decided to say nothing until they heard him preach again.

On the third Sunday, the pastor preached for 90 minutes. The elders agreed that was too long and asked the pastor what was going on.

"I was having problems with my dentures and couldn't talk very long the last two Sundays," the preacher said. "I had to do something, so this morning I borrowed my wife's teeth. Then I just couldn't stop talking."

—D. Arndt
Imlay City, Michigan

Gone Fishin'

WILLIE AND FRANK went fishing one Sunday but didn't have much luck. Willie said, "You know, I feel bad being out here when I ought to be in church."

Frank replied, "Well, I couldn't have gone to church to keep you company anyway. My wife's sick."

—Wilson Senn
Newberry, South Carolina

Hear All About It

A CHURCH BULLETIN informed parishioners that the minister would give a sermon on the topic of gossip—followed by the hymn I Love to Tell the Story.

Food for Thought

A YOUNG PASTOR announced nervously, "I will take for my text the words, 'And they fed five men with 5,000 loaves of bread and 2,000 fishes'."

At this misquotation, an old parishioner said, "That's no miracle. I could do that myself."

The next Sunday, the preacher announced the same text. This time he got it right. "And they fed 5,000 men on 5 loaves of bread and 2 fishes." He waited a moment, then leaned over the pulpit and asked the old parishioner, "And could you do that, too, Mr. Smith?"

"Of course I could," Mr. Smith replied.

"And how would you do it?" the preacher asked.

Mr. Smith answered, "With the leftovers from last Sunday."　　*—Jean Getka*
Sharon, Wisconsin

Barking Up the Wrong Tree

ONE of my nephews was out for a walk with his mother when a dog in a fenced yard began barking at them.

Trying to reassure the frightened child, his mother said soothingly, "There's an old proverb—barking dogs never bite."

Unconvinced, the lad asked, "Does the dog know that proverb?"

—J. Hampsch
Los Angeles, California

He Got the Whole Load

A PREACHER LOOKED out from the pulpit one Sunday morning and was shocked to see only one parishioner. He looked down at the cowboy and said, "Well, son, since we're the only ones here, why don't we forgo services today?"

The cowboy replied, "Sir, if I took a whole load of hay out to feed the cows and only one showed up, I'd still feed her."

This so inspired the preacher that he gave a sermon like he'd never given before. For the next 2 hours, the word of God flowed from him.

When he finally finished, he looked at the cowboy and said, "Well, what did you think of that?"

The cowboy replied, "Well, sir, I don't mean any disrespect, but if that one cow showed up, I sure wouldn't give her the whole load."　　*—Greg Smoker*
Wanatah, Indiana

Skunked Again

A MINISTER called the local sheriff to report a dead skunk in his driveway.

The harried sheriff said rudely, "We're too busy to be bothered by such trivial matters. Don't you preachers look after the dead?"

"Yes," came the dignified reply. "But first we notify the next of kin."

Chapter Five

Potpourri

Who says a good joke has to be categorized? Here are some good clean gems that range far and wide in subject matter.

Didn't Cotton To Work

TWO BOLL WEEVILS went out into the world to make their fortunes. The first boll weevil worked hard and became successful and rich. The second was lazy and not a bit industrious. That made him the lesser of two weevils.   —M. Horn
Crawfordsville, Indiana

Here, There, Everywhere

THE PREACHER told me the other day I should be thinking about the Hereafter. I told him, "I do, all the time. No matter where I am—in the parlor, upstairs, in the kitchen or in the basement—I'm always asking myself, 'Now, what am I here after'?"   —*Marv Reif*
Frankenmuth, Michigan

Facing the Facts

A LITTLE BOY asked his grandfather, "What's the difference between being a kid and being a grandpa?"

"Well, son, when I was a kid like you, I used to make faces in the mirror," the old man said. "Now the mirror gets even."

It Pays to Be Honest

A BUS PASSENGER returned to the ticket window and told the clerk, "You gave me the wrong change a few minutes ago."

"Sorry, sir," the agent said. "You should have called my attention to it before you walked away."

"You mean you can't correct it now?" the passenger asked.

"It's too late, sir."

"Oh, that's okay," the passenger said. "You gave me $5 too much."

Working His Way Up

A MAN WHO had just lost his job was chatting with a friend.

"Why did the foreman fire you?" the friend asked.

"Oh, you know how foremen are. They're always standing around with their hands in their pockets, watching everybody else work."

"Sure," the friend said. "Everybody knows that. But why did your foreman fire you?"

"Jealousy," the first man said. "All the other workers thought I was the foreman."

Can't Take It With You?

AN OLD MISER called his doctor, his lawyer and his pastor to his deathbed.

"They say you can't take it with you, but I'm going to," the dying man said. "I've got three envelopes here, each containing $30,000 cash. I want you to throw them into my casket just before it's closed."

At the funeral, each man tossed in his envelope. After the service, the pastor confessed, "I needed money for the church, so I took $10,000 out of my envelope."

The doctor said, "I, too, must confess. I'm building a clinic, and I took $20,000 out of my envelope."

"Gentlemen, I'm most ashamed of you," the lawyer said. "I threw in a check for the full amount."

—*G.M. Schmitt*
Mendota, Illinois

A Devilish Predicament

WHILE ARGUING with St. Peter about baseball, Satan made a proposal—a game pitting St. Peter's select team from the heavenly host against the Devil's own hand-picked boys.

"Very well," St. Peter agreed. "But I hope you realize that we have all the good players and the best coaches, too."

"I know," Satan said. "But we have all the umpires."

Keep Your Pants On

FOUR-YEAR-OLD Chester came in from playing and showed his mother a large tear in his trousers. She asked him to take them off, then went to the sewing room to mend them. When she finished, Chester was nowhere to be found.

The tot's mother heard someone moving around in the basement, so she went to the top of the stairs and called, "Are you running around down there without your pants on?"

"No, ma'am," a deep voice answered. "I'm just reading the meter."

Smoke Signal

A SPIRITUALIST received a message from her dead husband, asking her to send him a pack of cigarettes. "Where shall I send them?" she asked a friend. "He didn't give an address."

"Well," said the friend, "notice that he didn't ask for matches." —*Herb Schaefer Union Grove, Wisconsin*

Blame It on Eve

A WOMAN lecturer looked out over her audience and asked, "Where would man be today were it not for woman?" After a dramatic pause, she repeated loudly, "Again I ask, where would man be today were it not for woman?"

From the rear a male voice answered, "In the Garden of Eden."

It's Dog Eat Dog

A FELLOW was drinking coffee in a cafe when another man came in and asked, "Who owns that big police dog outside?" The coffee-drinker snarled, "I do. What's it to you?"

"He's dead," the other man said. "My dog killed him."

The police dog's owner was stunned. "That dog has never lost a fight," he said. "What kind of dog do you have?"

"A Chihuahua."

"How could a Chihuahua kill a police dog?"

"Well," the other man said, "he got stuck in his throat." —*M. Horn Crawfordsville, Indiana*

Cup O' Joe

AT BREAKFAST one morning, a man told his wife, "This coffee tastes like mud." She replied, "What do you expect? It was ground this morning." —*Rita Esser Arpin, Wisconsin*

Fill 'er Up

A TOURIST driving through Alabama saw a large sign at a gas station that read, "Mississippi State Line 2 Miles Ahead—Last Chance for 28¢ Gas". He pulled in and had his tank filled.

As the attendant handed over his change, the driver asked, "By the way, how

"I'm returning this fat-free, sugar-free, sodium-free, cholesterol-free cereal. The box was empty."

much does gas cost in Mississippi?"

The Alabaman replied, "Twenty-four cents."

Enjoy the Show

A YOUNG MAN was just about to sit down in one of a pair of empty seats in a very crowded theater when he was abruptly pushed off balance by a woman trailing him with her husband. Before the young man could recover, the couple had plopped into the seats.

"Sorry, my friend," the woman's husband said. "We beat you."

"That's quite all right," replied the young man. "I hope you and your mother enjoy the show."

Fish Story

ALWAYS REMEMBER that what is sushi in one establishment, is bait in another.
—*Stuart Robertshaw*
La Crosse, Wisconsin

What's in a Name?

A MAN was pulled over for speeding. The patrol officer, pad in hand, snapped, "Okay, what's your name?"

"Mustapha Toktobolot Dzhelalalshade," the driver replied.

"Well," the policeman said slowly, pocketing his pad, "don't let me catch you speeding again."

Hitting It on The Head

THE LIST of speakers was rather long, and some were known to be long-winded. The toastmaster announced that each speaker would be limited to 2 minutes. He'd rap his gavel when the 2 minutes were up.

The first speaker was still going strong after 2 minutes...and 5...and 10. Nearby, guests frantically signaled the toastmaster to lower the gavel. He finally did, but in his confusion he banged his hammer on the head of the man sitting next to him.

As the victim slipped under the table, he muttered, "Hit me again. I can still hear him."

Troubling Advice

A DOCTOR told his patient, "If you sing at the top of your voice for half an hour a day, you won't be troubled by chest complaints in your old age."

The patient replied, "If I do that in *my* neighborhood, I won't be troubled by old age, either."

Getting His Digs In

AN IRISH revolutionary serving time in prison received a letter from his wife. Because of his absence, she wrote, she'd have to dig the garden herself.

"Bridget, whatever you do, please don't dig the garden," Pat wrote back. "That's where the guns are buried."

The letter was duly censored, and before long, soldiers came and dug up Pat's garden from end to end.

Worried by the incident, Bridget wrote to Pat, asking what she should do. Pat's reply was short and to the point: "Put in the spuds."

Hand Signaling Would Be Tough

A POLICEMAN stopped a woman for a minor infraction. After the problem was resolved, he noticed she had a dog on the seat beside her.

"Does that dog have a license?" the officer asked.

"No," the woman answered. "He doesn't need one. I do all the driving."

A Cursory Glance

A BLACKSMITH had just put a horseshoe on the anvil to cool when a stranger walked into his shop. The stranger saw the horseshoe and walked over for a closer look. He started to pick it up and immediately dropped it.

"What's the matter?" the blacksmith asked the star-tled man. "Is it hot?"

"No," the stranger said. "It just doesn't take me long to look at a horseshoe."

—Harold Shell
Chalmers, Indiana

Fair is Fair

TWO IRISHMEN were sent out to cut a hole in the ice with a cross-cut saw. They'd never sawed through ice before. They just stood there, looking first at the ice, then at the saw. Finally Pat took a penny out of his pocket and said, "Now, let's be fair. Heads or tails—who goes below?" —Monica Fisher
Overton, Nebraska

Casting Fish

BOB'S fishing trip had been a flop. On his way home, he stopped at the local fish market and asked the clerk to throw five of his biggest fish to him.

"Throw 'em?" the clerk said. "What for?"

"So I can tell my wife I caught 'em," Bob replied. "I may be a lousy fisherman, but I'm not a liar."

—Louise Eppers
Fort Madison, Iowa

A Meal Fit for a Dog

A RESTAURANT patron couldn't finish the big steak she'd ordered, so she asked the waiter to wrap it up for her dog.

"I don't have a dog," she confided to her companions after the waiter left. "But now I can have a steak sandwich for lunch tomorrow."

After a few minutes, the waiter returned with a big paper bag and handed it to her. "I found a lot of leftover steak on other plates, too," he said, "so I wrapped them all together for you."

Life in the Slow Lane

"WHAT AM I supposed to do with this?" a motorist asked when the court clerk hand-

"It's the maitre d'…is everything all right?"

ed him a receipt for his traffic fine.

"Keep it," the clerk advised. "When you get 10 of them, you get a bicycle."

Strike Up The Band

A MAN told his doctor that whenever he put his hat on, he heard music. The doctor solved the problem by removing the man's hat and taking out the band.

—Eva Vale
Cottage Grove, Wisconsin

Waddle He Ask Next?

A DUCK walked into a feed store and asked for duck feed. The owner said that he didn't have any.

The next day, the duck came back and asked for duck feed again. The owner said he still didn't have any and told the duck to stop pestering him.

The third day, the duck came in again and asked for duck feed. The owner said he didn't have it and that if the duck came in again, he'd nail his webs to the floor.

The next day, the duck came back and asked the owner if he had any nails. "No," the owner said. "Okay," the duck said. "Do you have any duck feed?"

—Norma Foertsch
Evanston, Indiana

Here Comes a Gusher

A TEXAS oil man was in the dentist's chair. After a thorough examination, the dentist said, "Your teeth are in great shape. I can't think of a thing to do."

"Drill anyway," the Texan said. "I feel lucky today."

With Friends Like Him...

A COUPLE of mountain climbers crested a hill and came face to face with a grizzly bear. One climber sat down, took off his hiking boots and put on tennis shoes. His friend said, "You think you can outrun that bear?"

"I'm not thinking of outrunning the bear," the man replied. "I just want to outrun *you.*"
—Hank Endress
Wyoming, Illinois

All the Ins And Outs

DO YOU KNOW the difference between an in-law and an outlaw? The outlaw is wanted.
—*Dean Bresley*
Ord, Nebraska

Wasn't What She Had in Mind

A MAN and his wife noticed the couple next door kissing passionately on the porch. "Why can't you do that?" the wife asked. "Don't be silly," her husband replied. "I hardly know the woman."
—*Joyce Hargens*
Miller, South Dakota

Out on the Town

A MIDDLE-AGED COUPLE was eating supper one evening when the woman turned to her husband and said, "You know, I think we're getting into a rut. Every day we do the same thing. You come home from work, you read the paper, we eat supper, we watch television and we go to bed.

We should do something different, something exciting—go out and kick up our heels and do what we enjoy."

The good husband thought about this for a few minutes, then replied, "You know, I believe you're right. What do you say we do that very thing tonight? We'll go out and paint the town red, we'll kick up our heels like you wouldn't believe, and we'll do what we enjoy. And if you get home before I do, leave the porch light on."
—*Earl Kaiser*
Cadott, Wisconsin

Implements Of Affection

WHAT DID the wagon say to the tractor? "Pull me closer, John Deere!"
—*Chuck Kantner*
Wapakoneta, Ohio

A Rare Compliment

A DINER ordered his steak well-done, but it arrived so rare it was almost raw. The furious customer growled at the waiter, "I said 'well-done'. Didn't you hear me?"

"Yes, I did, sir," the waiter replied. "And I want to thank you. We don't get many compliments around here."

Students Wanted

A PROSPECTIVE college student and his father were touring the campus with a professor. The father asked the professor, "Just how many students do you have here?"

The professor pondered the question for a minute, then answered, "I'd say about one in a hundred."

They Bitin' Today?

A FISHERMAN is a guy who thinks a fish should bite on a fancy lure just because he did. —*Donna Ragsdale Union City, Tennessee*

A New Muffler... Over-Easy

A MECHANIC took a buddy to a coffee shop and told him, "Watch me have some fun with the waitress." Then he ordered two headlights, two mud flaps and two exhaust pipes.

The waitress wrote down the order and gave it to the cook. "Oh," the cook said. "He wants two eggs, two pancakes and two sausage links. Take him a bowl of bean soup."

"But he didn't order bean soup," the waitress said.

"Tell him to gas up while he's waiting on his parts." —*Donna Eckel Greensburg, Indiana*

But It's a Lucky Number

THREE MEN were sitting in a hospital waiting room while their wives gave birth. A nurse came out and told the first man, "Your wife just had twins."

"That's funny," he said. "I play for the Twins baseball team."

Then another nurse came out and told the second man he was the father of triplets.

"That's strange," he said. "I work for Three Sons, Inc."

At that, the third man fainted. The nurse asked what was wrong with him.

"I guess he's worried," one of the new fathers said. "He works for 7-Up." —*Earl Swanson Deer Creek, Minnesota*

Way Down In Dixie?

TWO ALASKANS spent their summer vacation in northernmost Maine and had the time of their lives. As they were leaving, one of them told their host, "Thank you so much. Now I know what they mean by Southern hospitality!"

—Richard Woody
Crawfordsville, Indiana

Starch With That?

RECENTLY, I saw this sign at a dry cleaner's: "We do not tear your clothes with huge machinery. We do it by hand." —Charles Volz
Benton, Missouri

Four for Fore

A GOLF FOURSOME was having trouble getting onto the links.

"Can't get the four of you off today, sir," the clubhouse clerk said. "We're really crowded."

"What if Ben Crenshaw, Jack Nicklaus, Hale Irwin and Greg Norman showed up?" one of the quartet asked.

"Oh! We'd have to give them a round," came the reply.

"Well, they're playing in the Masters. We'll just take their spot."

Which Animal Lives Longest?

WHAT has more lives than a cat? A frog—he croaks every night. —Henry, Emma and Luci Teague
Greenwood, South Carolina

Weighting for The Truth

A MAN and his wife were in a drugstore, waiting for a clerk, when they spotted a scale. They walked over to it and the woman climbed aboard.

Out popped a card that said, "You are warm-hearted, lovable, understanding and an excellent cook."

Reading over her shoulder, her husband remarked, "It didn't get your weight right, either."

—Mrs. Cecil Seggelke
Warsaw, Illinois

Proper Use of The Airwaves

WHEN A WOMAN in a small Iowa town celebrated her 90th birthday, the Chamber of Commerce offered her a free airplane trip to New York. She turned the offer down in no uncertain terms.

"Not on your life," she vowed. "You'll never get me up in one of those newfangled machines. I'm going to stay right at home and watch television, just like the good Lord intended us to do."

Earned Her Wings

I MARRIED an angel. She's always up in the air and harping about things.
—*Donald Schneider*
Willmar, Minnesota

"I'm wearing my vertical stripe dress and you *still* lie!"

Practice Makes Perfect

A GOLFER on the first tee blasted a mighty drive that was picked up by the wind and floated 465 yards down the fairway. The ball plopped onto the green, rolled up to the pin and dropped into the cup.

"Not bad," his partner commented. "Now I'll take *my* practice shot and we can get started."

Goin' Like 60

I'M NOT only getting older, I'm slowing down. Last week it took me an hour and a half to watch *60 Minutes.*
—*Harold Shell*
Chalmers, Indiana

That Seat Taken?

NICK was lucky enough to get a ticket to the big football game, but his seat was near the top row. He spotted one empty seat near the 50-yard line and made a bee-line for it at halftime.

Nick approached the man sitting next to the empty seat and asked if he could use it. "Oh, yes," the man said. "This was my wife's seat, but she died."

"I'm sorry to hear that," Nick said. "But didn't one of your friends or relatives want to use her ticket?"

"Well, I offered," the man said. "But they were all going to her funeral."
—*George Lonsdorf*
Merrill, Wisconsin

That's Why He's a Pro

"ARNOLD PALMER played here last year," the caddie told the golfer as they approached a lagoon shot.

"What would *he* have used on this hole?" the golfer asked.

"Playing your game, sir, probably an old ball."

Luck O' the Irish

AN IRISHMAN in Boston was out of work and applied for a job at the zoo. He was told the zoo's baboon had died.

The man's job would be putting on the creature's tanned hide and entertaining the children who came to see him.

The Irishman took the job and played the part well, until some boys threw stones at him. He grabbed the bars and shook them so vigorously that the door between his cage and the lion's swung open.

Before the baboon could close the door, an old lion walked in. The baboon climbed up the bars of his cage, yelling, "Help! Help!"

The lion stood on his hind legs, grabbed the baboon's legs, and muttered, "Come down, you fool. You're not the only Irishman out of a job."

Be Mine

MY DAUGHTER-IN-LAW asked her husband, "Did you buy your sweetheart a valentine?" He quickly answered, "Yes. Do I have to buy you one, too?"

—E. Baldwin
Winchester, Indiana

Happy Birthday To...*Who*?

A COUPLE wanted to sur-
prise their neighbor on his birthday, so they dialed and sang *Happy Birthday* into the phone. When they finished, they discovered they had the wrong number.

"Don't let that bother you," the stranger told them. "You folks can use the practice."

What Goes Around...

FRED was a truck driver who stopped at the same diner every day for coffee and a doughnut. One morning, the waitress saw him pull into the lot, so she put his coffee and doughnut on the counter for him.

Just as Fred sat down, two motorcycles roared up, and the riders walked in. One grabbed Fred's coffee and the other took his doughnut. Fred just paid the waitress and walked out.

One cyclist said to the other, "He isn't much of a man, is he?"

The waitress, who was looking out the window, said, "He isn't much of a truck driver, either. He just ran over two motorcycles in the parking lot."

—Avery Rich
Durham, North Carolina

Revenge Is Whose?

A TEACHER ran a red light and was pulled over by a policeman, who took her before a judge.

"So you're a school-teacher," the judge said. "That's fine. Madam, I've waited for years to have a schoolteacher standing before me. Now, sit down at the table and write 500 times, 'I went through a red light'."

You Can't Please Critics

DON'T CRITICIZE your wife. If she were perfect, she would have married better.

An Adequate Replacement

A MAN was driving down a dark road when a cat bolted from a yard and ran right in front of his car. The driver couldn't stop in time.

He gently carried the limp animal up to the house. A white-haired lady answered the door.

"My good woman," the man said, "I'm afraid that I've run over your cat. It was unavoidable. But I'd very much like to replace it."

"I see," the woman replied. "How are you at catching mice?"

A Dogged Competitor

MOREY was going to be late for Harry's weekly poker game. Instead of delaying the game, Harry suggested that his dog be allowed to play the fourth hand until Morey arrived.

"Your *dog*?" said one of his buddies.

"Sure," Harry said. "He's a terrific card player."

The others were skeptical, but decided to give the dog a chance. To their surprise, the dog really was a good player and even won a few small pots.

When Morey finally arrived, he watched in astonishment as the dog finished his last hand and left the table.

"Wow," Morey said as he sat down. "A dog playing poker! That was really amazing."

"Not really," said one of

the players. "Every time he had a good hand, he wagged his tail."

Their True Colors?

A TEENAGER asked her mother, "Why do some of your friends color their hair?"

Her mother replied, "Because they'd rather dye than show their age."

Look Again

The only known cure for love at first sight is a second look. —*Charles Porter*
Odon, Indiana

It's a Logical Choice

AN OLD GENT was taking a walk on a golf course when he spotted a frog. The frog said, "If you pick me up and rub my back, I'll turn into a young gal." The man picked the frog up and put it in his pocket.

The frog called, "Didn't you hear? I said if you rub my back, I'll turn into a young gal!"

"I heard you," the man said. "But at my age I'd just as soon have a talking frog."
—*Ray Seeley*
Schofield, Wisconsin

Monthly Statement

A WOMAN was looking for a new outfit at the mall. "I don't know much about fashion," she told the sales clerk. "The only fashion statement I've ever made is, 'I can't afford it'."

No Use Crying Foul

TWO COLLEGE football teams with a long-standing rivalry were locked in a close, hard-fought game.

Tensions were running high. A foul was called, and the referee gave the offending team a 10-yard penalty.

The team captain bawled out the referee with a blistering tirade, finishing it off with a firm, "I think you stink!"

The referee added 15 more yards to the penalty. Then he pointed down the field and told the captain, "See how I smell from there."

"This is the lady behind you...the label is sticking out of the neck of your dress..."

There Must Have Been a Re-Districting

PAT AND MIKE were friendly adversaries and never missed an opportunity for one-upmanship.

At election time, Mike was running for alderman and was trying to get Pat's vote.

"I wouldn't vote for you if you were St. Peter himself," Pat said.

Mike shot back, "If I were St. Peter, you wouldn't be in my ward."

Out of Order

THE DISTRAUGHT taxpayer handed the IRS agent his tax return and a large check.

"Those guys in Washington are a heartless bunch," he complained. "They cleaned out my bank account!"

"Cheer up," the IRS man said. "Remember what Benjamin Franklin said—nothing is certain but death and taxes."

"Maybe so," the taxpayer grumbled. "But I wish they came in that order."

She'd Rather Tune It Out

A MAN appeared at the front door and announced, "Madam, I'm the piano tuner."

"I didn't send for a tuner," the pianist said.

"I know, lady," the man said. "Your neighbor did."

—Gertrude Oetterer
Finlayson, Minnesota

Alive and Kicking

THE DOCTOR asked his 80-year-old patient how he'd been feeling.

"Well," the old fellow said, "I'm still kicking, but I'm not raising as much dust as I used to."

How's That Again?

UNCLE JOHN'S hearing had begun to deteriorate, and his doctor recommended a hearing aid. But Uncle John thought they were too expensive. Instead, he inserted an earplug from a portable radio and fastened the end of the wire under his necktie.

A friend knew what Uncle John had done and told him, "That's not connected to anything. How can it help you hear?"

"Oh, you'd be surprised," Uncle John said. "Whenever anybody sees it, they talk louder."

What Goes Around Comes Around

A WOMAN told her husband she had to fire the new maid.

"Why?" the man asked.

"She was sneaking off with a pair of towels," his wife said.

"Which ones?"

His wife replied, "The ones you got from the Holiday Inn in Des Moines."

—Mike Hennenfent
Smithshire, Illinois

How Old Are You?

YOU KNOW you're getting older when...

- The gleam in your eyes is from the sun hitting your bifocals.
- Your children begin to look middle-aged.
- You decide to procrastinate, but never get around to it.
- Your back goes out more than you do.
- You burn the midnight oil when you're up past 9 p.m.
- The little old lady you help across the street is your wife. —*Virginia Marshall South Zanesville, Ohio*

Improving the Odds

A MAN TOOK his talking dog into a bar on Abraham Lincoln's birthday and began bragging about the mutt's knowledge of history. Before getting his dog to perform, he picked up a few bets from the spectators.

Then the man turned to his dog and said, "Now, tell us, what day was Lincoln born?" The dog didn't say a word.

Again the man urged the dog to talk. He asked him a dozen questions about the great president and got nothing but silence. In disgust, he paid off his bets and left the bar.

As he drove away, the man asked the dog, "Why didn't you say anything back there? You cost me 20 bucks!"

"I was thinking ahead," the dog replied. "Think of the odds you'll get when we go back on Washington's birthday."

Here's My Order

AN ELDERLY MAN asked his wife to bring him a dish of ice cream. "I can do that," she said.

"You'd better write this down, because I want chocolate syrup on it," he said.

"I can remember," she said.

"You'd better write it down, because I want nuts on it, too," he added.

"I can remember," she assured him.

A while later, the wife returned from the kitchen with a piece of toast. Her husband said, "See, I told you you'd forget the jelly."

—*Sharon Fritchley Gentryville, Indiana*

Neither a Borrower Nor a Lender Be

DID YOU hear about the man who had too many relatives coming to visit? He solved the problem by borrowing money from the rich ones and loaning it to the poor ones. Now none of them come back.

—Jacob Rader
Defiance County, Ohio

Typographical Terrors

TYPOGRAPHICAL errors can be a nightmare not only for newspapers, but for their advertisers. Consider this ad from a small-town paper and subsequent attempts to correct it.

Monday: FOR SALE—R.D. Jones has one sewing machine for sale. Phone 555-0707 after 7 p.m. and ask for Mrs. Kelly, who lives with him cheap.

Tuesday: NOTICE—We regret having erred in R.D. Jones' ad yesterday. It should have read: "One sewing machine for sale. Cheap. Phone 555-0707 and ask for Mrs. Kelly, who lives with him after 7 p.m."

Wednesday: NOTICE—R.D. Jones has informed us that he has received several annoying telephone calls because of the error we made in his classified ad yesterday. His ad stands correct as follows: "FOR SALE—R.D. Jones has one sewing machine for sale. Cheap. Phone 555-0707 and ask for Mrs. Kelly, who loves with him."

Thursday: NOTICE—I, R.D. Jones, have no sewing machine for sale. I smashed it. Don't call 555-0707, as the telephone has been taken out. I have not been carrying on with Mrs. Kelly. Until yesterday she was my housekeeper, but she quit.

Ear Today, Gone Tomorrow

A MAN was sawing a limb off a tree when he accidentally cut off his ear, so he climbed down to look for it. Another man walked past and asked what he was looking for.

"My ear," the man said.

"There's an ear," said the passerby, pointing. "Is that yours?"

"Nope," the man said. "Mine had a pencil behind it."

—Marie Oxley
Greenfield, Iowa

Odds Are...

WHAT do you call a tax on people who did poorly in math class? A state lottery.

—*Eugene Goering*
Platte Center, Nebraska

A Good Provider

"WELL, young man, you've asked permission to marry my daughter," the fastidious father said. "Can you support a family?"

"No, sir, I can't," the would-be groom replied. "I was only planning to support your daughter. The rest of you will have to get along the best you can."

—*John Hoyt, Galena, Ohio*

Must Be Fertile Ground

A DISC JOCKEY on a country radio station had the after-midnight shift and took requests from his audience all night long. About 2 a.m., a listener tried to call him, but got the wrong number and woke up a farmer in Georgia.

"Do you have *A Sweetheart in Tennessee*?" the caller asked.

The sleepy farmer replied, "Naw, I got a wife and 10 kids in Georgia."

"Is that a record?" the caller asked.

"Don't know about that," the farmer said, "but it's way above average."

—*Mildred Hiatt*
Anderson, Indiana

It Pays to Listen

AN ELDERLY MAN finally decided to get a hearing aid. Some time later, he stopped at the store where he'd bought it. The beaming manager greeted him and said, "Your relatives must be happy that your hearing is so much better."

"Oh, I ain't told 'em," the old-timer chuckled. "I've just been sitting around the house, listening. You know, I've heard enough to change my will twice already."

—*Mrs. R.J. Kalisek*
Howells, Nebraska

Painful Sight

TWO MEN were seated on a bus when one noticed the other's eyes were closed.

"What's the matter, Bill?" he asked. "Are you feeling ill?"

FIREWOOD $75 CORD NOW TAKING FUTURE ORDERS

"No, I'm all right," his friend replied. "It's just that I hate to see all these ladies standing."

It Takes One to Know One

"I'M NEVER playing golf with George again," a man told his wife. "Why, that cheat found his last ball one foot away from the green!"

"Well, that could happen," his wife said.

Her husband replied, "Not when I've got the ball in my pocket." —*Joyce Hargens Miller, South Dakota*

Stop the Presses!

A VETERAN sportswriter sat in the press box after the last game of the World Series, filing his story for the newspaper. Next to him sat a very young writer who was covering his first World Series.

The young man, intent on creating some memorable prose, pointed to the setting sun and asked his grizzled colleague, "Is that the west?"

"If it isn't," the old-timer answered, "you've got one heck of a scoop on your hands."

Going to the Dogs

DO YOU KNOW how to turn a cute little poodle into a pit bull? Marry her.

—Robert Lange
West Burlington, Iowa

Time for a Change

TWO WOMEN were discussing reincarnation. "I don't know whether I'd rather come back wealthy or gorgeous," the first woman mused.

"Well," replied the second, "either way it'll be a change."

You Can't Win

ONE DAY a letter addressed to God arrived at the post office. The postmaster was curious and opened it. The letter read:

"Dear God, my mama works very hard to make ends meet for us children. We have no daddy, and we need $500. Please, God, send it soon."

The good folks at the post office were moved by the letter. They took up a collection of $300 and mailed it to the little boy. A few days later, another letter addressed to God arrived. It read:

"Dear God, thank you for the $300. But next time, could you please deliver the money in person? The post office shorted us $200."

—Johnnie Herter
Wausau, Florida

John Wilkes Who?

A FELLOW was a little slow and needed a job. His wife saw an ad in the paper for deputy sheriff. Thinking it was a Barney Fyfe type of job, she encouraged him to apply.

The sheriff told the applicant he'd have to take a little test. "What is one and one?" the sheriff asked.

"Eleven," the man replied.

The sheriff rolled his eyes and went to the next question. "What two days of the week begin with the letter 'T'?"

"Today and tomorrow," the man answered.

Frustrated, the sheriff said, "I've got one more question for you. Who shot Abraham Lincoln?"

"I don't know," the man said.

To get rid of this dull fellow, the sheriff said, "Go home and study up on that question."

When the man returned home, his wife asked whether he got the job. "Yep," he said. "They've already put me to work on a murder case."

—Leanna Adler
Rudolph, Ohio

Room for Improvement

A TEXAN was escorting an Englishman through part of the Lone Star State. Pointing to one of the endless plains, the Texan boasted, "You know, your whole country could fit into one corner of Texas."

"Yes," the Englishman agreed, "and it would do wonders for the place."

It Makes Sense

THE census-taker asked the homemaker her name. "It's Ann Smith."

"And your age, please?" Mrs. Smith hesitated. "Have the Hills next door given you their ages?" she asked.

"Yes, they have," the census-taker said.

"I'm the same age they are," Mrs. Smith said.

"Very good," the census-taker said. "I'll just write on the form that Ann Smith is as old as the Hills."

I'll Have No Lip From You

A DUCK walked into a drugstore and asked for a Chapstick. When the clerk got it off the shelf, the duck asked her to put it on his bill.

—Norma Foertsch
Evanston, Indiana

They Didn't Call It 'The Mess' for Nothing

A RESTAURANT OWNER was carefully checking the work of his new cook.

"You say you were an army cook during the war?" the owner asked doubtfully.

"Yes, sir," the cook said. "I cooked for the officers' mess for over 2 years and was wounded three times."

"Huh," his boss said. "You're lucky they didn't kill you."

On a Tight Schedule

BEFORE the fall of communism, Russians had to wait in line for everything. In 1993, a Russian ordered a car from a Moscow dealer and was told it would be ready May 20, 1996.

"Would that be in the morning or the afternoon?" the purchaser inquired.

The dealer nearly lost his temper. "Comrade, you're lucky to get a car at all," he said. "And anyway, it's 3 years from now. What possible difference could it make?"

The Russian replied, "The plumber's coming in the morning."

—*Craig Hathaway*
Milwaukee, Wisconsin

"We get a lot of rug divot problems during the rainy season."

Is That in the Bible?

A SENIOR CITIZENS' center serves meals cafeteria-style, with one line for the handicapped and one for those without handicaps. The lines are marked "Cane" and "Able".

Worth Fussing Over

A WOMAN is someone who makes a big fuss over nothing—and then marries him.
—*Charles Porter*
Odon, Indiana

Breath of Fresh Air

A GROUP of church women were waiting to be admitted to Heaven when St. Peter approached. "Ladies, I must apologize for the inconvenience, but Heaven is full," he said. "You'll have to wait below until our new wing is finished."

Several days later, St. Peter got a frantic call from the Devil himself. "You've got to get these women out of here!" Satan complained. "With their bake sales, rummage sales and bazaars, they're only $50 short of air-conditioning the place!"
—*G.M. Schmitt*
Mendota, Illinois

Paid Union Scale?

MY brother-in-law told me he once was paid $15 for singing. I was astonished. "Somebody paid you $15 to sing?" I asked.

"Yep," he said. "Five dollars to start and $10 to quit."
—*Ralph Dodds*
North Branch, Michigan

Dogs Welcome

A MAN wrote to a hotel to ask if his dog would be allowed to stay there. A few days later, he received the following reply:

"Dear Sir, I've been in the hotel business for over 30 years. I've never had to call the police to eject a disorderly dog in the small hours of the morning. No dog has ever attempted to pass a bad check. Never has a dog set the bedclothes on fire from smoking. And I've never found a hotel towel in a dog's suitcase. Your dog is welcome.

"P.S. If he will vouch for you, you can come, too."

An Instructional Exercise

DO YOU KNOW why the chicken crossed the road? To show the possums it can be done. —*Judy Renbarger Greentown, Indiana*

She's Feeling Superior

AN elderly mother superior wasn't feeling well, and the other nuns insisted she see a doctor. After the examination, the doctor took the other sisters aside and told them the mother superior had circulation problems.

"The best thing for her would be a little drink each morning," he said.

"Oh, no," the sisters protested. "There's no way she'd ever drink alcohol."

"All right," the doctor said. "Then give her a glass of fresh milk from your cow each morning and slip a little vodka in it." They took his advice, and the mother superior soon felt like herself again.

Years later, as the nuns gathered around the mother superior on her deathbed, they asked if she had any final wishes.

"Yes," she said. "Don't ever sell that cow."
—*Stewart Welch Tarpon Springs, Florida*

Taking Beauty to Another Level

A COUNTRY BUMPKIN and his son were making their first trip to the city. While sightseeing, they walked into a hotel and saw an elevator—something they'd never seen before.

They watched as a tired cleaning woman walked into the elevator. The door closed. Fifteen seconds later, the door opened and a beautiful, well-dressed woman emerged.

"Son," the father said, "next time we come to town, we've got to run your ma through that thing."
—*Mildred Hiatt Anderson, Indiana*

Doing the Bunny Hop

WHAT DO YOU CALL 100 rabbits dancing backward? A receding hare line.
—*M. Horn Crawfordsville, Indiana*

Happy Talk

I NEVER KNEW what real happiness was until I got married. And then it was too late. —*John Edinborough Gooding, Idaho*

Paradise Lost

A RANCHER was driving an Easterner over a barren section of West Texas scrubland. The sun was blistering hot. Suddenly a gaudy-looking bird ran in front of the car. The visitor was intrigued and asked about it.

"That's a bird of paradise," the rancher explained.

They drove the next mile in silence, until the visitor observed, "Pretty far from home, isn't he?"

"I've always wanted to meet you, too."

154

Chapter Six

Kids Can Be Clowns

**Small comments
from kids can
prompt big laughs
in adults.**

An Educated Guess?

A BOY and his sister ran from the barn to tell Mom the cat just had kittens—two boys and two girls. "How do you know what they are?" their mother asked. The boy said, "Well, Daddy picked them up and looked underneath, so it must be stamped on there somewhere."

—Rita Esser
Arpin, Wisconsin

The New Math

THE TEACHER asked her students, "If you had 10 potatoes and had to divide them among 12 people, how would you do it?" One child replied, "Mash 'em."

Beep...Beep... Beep...

A 4-YEAR-OLD was shopping with his father, looking for a birthday present for Mom. In the kitchenware aisle, they saw a rather large woman wearing a pocket pager. As they walked past her, the woman's pager began beeping. The boy grabbed his father and said, "Watch out, Dad. She's backing up!"

—Janet Geissler
Carthage, Illinois

Passing the Plate

A WOMAN asked her daughter, "Marilyn, were you a good little girl at church today?"

"Yes, Mother," Marilyn replied. "A man offered me a big plate of money and I said, 'No, thank you'."

Berry Good Idea

A WOMAN came home from a nearby farm with two buckets of cow manure for the garden.

"What's that for?" asked 6-year-old Kelly.

"The strawberries," Mom answered.

After staring at the buckets for a moment, Kelly asked, "Can I just have mine with whipped cream?"

Long Time Gone

BEFORE THE FALL of communism, a boy in

Moscow answered the door and found a stranger asking to see his father.

"He's not here," the boy said. "He's in outer space and won't be home until 11:32 a.m. tomorrow."

"And your mother?" the stranger asked.

"Heaven knows when she'll be back," the boy said. "She's standing in line at the butcher shop."

Bargain Hunter

A LITTLE GIRL, enchanted by her new baby cousin, asked her mother, "Can't we have a baby?"

"I don't believe so, darling," her mother replied. "They cost too much."

"How much?" the child inquired.

"Oh, about $4,000," her mother said.

The youngster thought for a moment, then said, "That's not very much, when you consider how long they last."

Doggone Right

THE CROWDED school bus pulled to the curb to make way for a speeding fire truck. The children were fascinated by the dalmatian seated beside the driver.

"Why did the firemen have that dog with them?" one child asked.

"To bark at the crowds and keep people out of the way," another child said.

"No, he's there for good luck," insisted a third.

The argument ended when one lad explained, "They use the dog to find the fire hydrant."

Gettin' Crowded In There

A LITTLE GIRL was nervous about her medical checkup, so the doctor did his best to put her at ease. As he looked in one ear, he said, "Ooh, I see Big Bird in there!" Then he looked in her mouth and said, "And I believe I see Kermit the Frog in there!"

Then the doctor put his stethoscope to the child's chest and said, "I think I can hear Barney in your heart."

"Oh, no, Doctor," the child said quickly. "I have Jesus in my heart. Barney's on my underwear."

—*Bruce Mottweiler*
Edwardsburg, Michigan

Daddy's Trick

LITTLE BILLY opened the door wide when his grandmother arrived. "Gee, Grandma, I'm glad to see you," he said. "Now Daddy can do his trick."

"What trick is that?" Grandma asked.

"Well," Billy said, "Daddy told Mommy that if you came to visit again, he'd start climbing the walls."

Using His Head

THE BRIGHT PUPIL looked long and hard at the question on his exam. It read, "State the number of tons of coal shipped out of the United States in any given year." After much thought, his face brightened and he wrote, "1492—none".

Believe It

A KINDERGARTEN teacher asked her pupils to share something about their parents. One child said, "Well, my mother's a Catholic and my father's a Jew."

"Wow!" said another child. "So what do you believe?"

"I believe in everything," the first child said.

"What do you mean, 'everything'?"

"You know," the child said, "Jesus Christ, Moses, Snow White—everything."

—Richard Woody
Crawfordsville, Indiana

Waiting Patiently

A TEACHER showed her grade school class a picture of *Whistler's Mother* and asked them to jot down their impressions of the painting. One boy wrote, "It's a nice old lady waiting for the repairman to bring back her TV set."

But That Was a Guaranteed Reservation

DURING the children's Christmas play at church, Joseph asked the innkeeper if he and Mary could have a room.

"No, we have no room," said the child playing the innkeeper.

Then he forgot his next line, so he quickly added,

"Some guys wear their caps forward, some backward...
I like to be different."

"But why don't you come on in and have a drink."

Let 'Er Rip

A LITTLE FELLOW got a late start for school one morning, so he took a short-cut. He snagged his pants on a barbed-wire fence, ripping a hole in the seat. He searched his pockets and found one safety pin. He pinned up his pants as best he could and hurried on.

School was already in session when he arrived. As he hung up his coat, the teacher said, "Johnny, I see you're a little behind."

"Yeah," Johnny said, "but if I'd had another pin you couldn't."   —*Leo Alger*
North Manchester, Indiana

Step On It

A MAN WAS SHOCKED when his son begged to be driven to school, only 3 blocks away, after a light snowfall.

"Drive you to school?" Dad exclaimed. "Danny, why do you suppose God gave you two feet?"

Danny quickly replied, "One for the brake, the other for the accelerator."

And That's a Promise

A CHILD sitting on Santa's

"We can get kids to read more if we outline each page so it looks like a TV screen."

lap looked up at him and asked, "Are you a politician?"

"Of course not," Santa replied. "Why would you think I'm a politician?"

"'Cause you always promise more than you deliver." —*Richard Woody Crawfordsville, Indiana*

Cow vs. Tractor

"MY FATHER can't decide whether to get a new cow or a new tractor," a farm boy told his city friend.

"He'd certainly look silly riding on a cow," the city boy said.

"Yeah," the farm boy said, "but he'd look a lot sillier milking a tractor."

That Dog Will Hunt

A MOTHER was concerned about her small son's habit of telling tall tales and asked her preacher for advice. He told her to bring the boy to his office. While the preacher was waiting, he dreamed up the tallest tale he could imagine.

When the boy arrived, the preacher said, "Son, one Sunday when I was preach-ing, a big grizzly bear came in the door and walked right down the aisle. Everyone was scared. No one knew what to do.

"Then a little terrier came in and bit the bear on the hind leg. When the bear turned, the dog grabbed the bear by the throat and killed it. The dog dragged the bear out of the church, and I went on with my sermon."

After a pause, the preacher said, "Do you believe that story?"

"Sure," the boy said. "That was my dog."
—*Bill Riggle Iowa City, Iowa*

Lying About His Age

A WOMAN approached an airline ticket counter with her little boy. A sign at the counter read: "Children 2 years old and under get a discount."

The woman asked for the discounted fare, but the clerk was suspicious. He turned to the boy and asked, "Do you know what happens to little boys who lie?"

"Yes, I do," the child replied. "They ride for half-fare."

Remember the Sabbath?

"PA'S NOT HOME," the youngster told the minister who came calling on Sunday afternoon. "He went over to the country club."

When the minister's face registered distress, the youngster hastily added, "Oh, he's not gonna play golf—not on Sunday. He just went over for a little game of poker."

Sounds Like a Swap

A SINCERE Sunday school teacher asked the children, "What can we do for God? He has done so much for us. He gave us his Son."

One little girl piped up, "I'll give him my brother."
—*Lois Schneider*
Arlington, South Dakota

Quite a Procession

A LITTLE GIRL took much too long returning from the store. When she got home, her worried mother asked, "What on earth took you so long?"

"I was watching the Devil's funeral," the girl replied.

"What do you mean?" her astonished mother asked.

"Well, I was watching the funeral cars go by, and a man next to me said the poor devil was only sick about a week."

Outsmarted

FOUR HIGH-SCHOOL boys with spring fever skipped their morning classes. After lunch, they told their teacher their car had a flat tire.

To their relief, she just smiled and said, "Well, you missed a test this morning, so take seats apart from each other and get out your notebooks."

When the boys had settled into the seats, the teacher said pleasantly, "Here's your first question. Which tire was flat?"

Three-Way Conversation?

AS TOMMY said his bedtime prayers, his mother said, "Honey, I can't hear you."

"That's okay," Tommy said. "I wasn't speaking to you." —*Louise Eppers*
Fort Madison, Iowa

That Explains It

RACHEL liked to help her mother with housework, so she was happy to set the table when Daddy's boss came for dinner. But when everyone sat down to eat, the boss didn't have any silverware.

"Rachel," Mother said, "why doesn't Mr. Smith have any silverware?"

"I didn't think he'd need any," Rachel explained. "Daddy says he always eats like a horse." —*Donald Erb*
Lafayette, Indiana

"How come you're *still* a student?"

"Why don't they just download this manual, and then we wouldn't have to keep thumbing through it?"

Putting It All Together

AFTER A WEEK at a dude ranch, the little girl came home and told her father excitedly, "Dad, I saw a man who makes horses!"

"Are you sure?" her father asked.

"Oh, yes!" she replied.

"He had one of the horses nearly finished when I saw him. He was just nailing on the feet."

Sealed In

TWO second-graders were walking home from school.

"Did you buy any Christmas seals?" Chris asked.

"No," replied Brad. "I wouldn't know what to feed them." —*Richard Woody Crawfordsville, Indiana*

It'll Take Time

A LITTLE BOY was lying in front of the fireplace, scribbling on a piece of paper. Suddenly he rushed into the kitchen with the paper and said, "Look, Mom, I've learned to write!"

"Well, what does it say?" his mother asked.

"I don't know," he said. "I haven't learned to read yet." —*Charles Shultz Jackson, Missouri*

Yesterday... Today...Tomorrow

A DETERMINED daycare instructor was trying to teach preschoolers the days of the week—without much success. After drilling them for several days, she again asked, "What day is today?"

As usual, no one knew. One youngster said, "Tuesday." Another said, "Monday."

"No, no, no!" the teacher said. "It's Thursday. Today is Thursday."

At that, a little girl held up her hand and complained, "Teacher, every day you change the answer." —*Jessie Drost Anderson, Indiana*

Let Dad Drive

FOUR CO-WORKERS were discussing what they hoped to get out of their new cars.

"Economy," said one man.

"Dependability," said the second.

"Styling," said the third.

They all turned to the fourth fellow, who was standing there with a grim expression. "What I'd most like to get out of my new car," he said, "is my teenage son."

Just Being Neighborly

"JIMMY," said Mother, "why don't you run across the street and see how old Mrs. Weiss is." A few minutes later, Jimmy returned and reported, "She says it's none of your business how old she is." —*Joyce Hargens Miller, South Dakota*

As Good as It Gets

A LITTLE GIRL told her friend, "I can be sick for nothing because my father's a doctor."

"That's nothing," her playmate replied. "I can be good for nothing because my father's a minister."

That's a Relief

WHEN a 6-year-old boy returned home from school, his mother asked about his day.

"Today the teacher asked me whether I had any brothers or sisters," the boy said. "I told her I was an only child."

"And what did she say, dear?"

"She said, 'Thank goodness'." —*Gertrude Oetterer Finlayson, Minnesota*

Take the Money And Run

THE SUNDAY SCHOOL teacher was trying to demonstrate the difference between right and wrong.

"All right, children, here's an example," she said. "If I were to go into a man's pocket and take his wallet with all his money, what would I be?"

A child in back answered, "His wife."

Anybody in There?

A LITTLE BOY was afraid of the dark. His mother told him not to worry, because God was with him wherever he went. When the boy went upstairs at bedtime, he opened the door to his darkened room and yelled, "God, if you're in there, would you throw out my pajamas?"
—*Elaine Dougherty Greenwood, Indiana*

Thanks, But No Thanks

FOR CHRISTMAS, my wife bought our 3-year-old grandson a construction toy. He'd get three or four pieces together, but every time he tried to add another, it would fall apart. After watching him do this several times, I asked, "Do you want Grandpa to help you?"

"Listen to that. The younger generation sure is soft."

"No thanks," he said. "I'm having enough trouble as it is."   —*LaVern Packel*
Columbus, Wisconsin

If the Shoe Fits...

A FIRST-GRADE teacher struggled mightily to get a little boy into his overshoes. When she finally succeeded, the boy said, "These aren't my boots."

The teacher struggled to get them off again, then put on the boy's shoes and tied them. Then the child said, "They're my sister's, but Mom says I have to wear them."   —*Arline Baird*
Central City, Nebraska

Cheap Transportation

A COLLEGE FRESHMAN was begging his father for a late-model car so he could drive to school with some dignity. "All the other fellows have practically new cars," he said.

One day his father had occasion to visit the college. As he drove around campus with his son, they passed a parking lot full of clunkers. Every single car looked ready to fall apart.

"These cars don't look new to me," the father observed.

"Oh, Dad," his exasperated son said. "That's the faculty parking lot."

"Isn't that sweet?
She's communicating that she doesn't like it."

Money Can't Buy Everything

OUR 6-YEAR-OLD was having a hard time minding his manners. Just before Mother's Day, he asked what kind of gift I wanted. I told him all I wanted was one day without fighting, bickering, yelling or any other bad behavior.

Philip looked at me with sad puppy-dog eyes and said, "Oh, Mom, can't we just buy you something?"

—Denise Hendrickx
Fergus Falls, Minnesota

Don't Give Up Yet

DURING a game of checkers, my little grandson looked up and said, "I'm gonna get beat."

I told him, "It's not over until the fat lady sings."

Eric replied, "Well, Grandma, I can hear her tuning her guitar." —E. Baldwin
Winchester, Indiana

Step On It, Doc

TWO YOUNG BOYS walked into the dentist's office. One faced him boldly and said, "Doc, I want a tooth taken out, and I don't want any gas 'cause I'm in a hurry."

"I must say you're a brave boy," the dentist said. "Which tooth is it?"

The boy turned to his silent friend and said, "Show him your tooth, Arthur."

Testing Teacher

TOMMY APPROACHED his teacher and asked, "Teacher, can a fellow be punished for something he hasn't done?"

"Of course not," the teacher said.

"Well, then," Tommy said, "I haven't done my arithmetic."

Lousy Mileage

A MAN ASKED a friend how much mileage he was getting out of his sporty new car. He thought about it and answered, "As near as I can figure, I get about 5 miles to the gallon. My teenager gets the other 20."

What's It Worth?

IT'S OFTEN SAID that children don't know the value of money. That's only partially true. They don't know the value of your money, but they know the value of theirs.

Show Her the Money

MY GRAND-NIECE came home from Sunday school and asked her mother what Heaven was like. Her mother explained what a wonderful place it was, and said no one needed money there because God didn't have any.

"He ought to," the little girl retorted. "I give him some every Sunday."
—Ray Henry
Richland Center, Wisconsin

Horse Trading

GEORGE WAS BORED with his pet turtle and decided to sell it. He put the turtle dish on a small table on the front porch, with a sign that read: "Turtle for sale, $1."

"George, you've got to learn to think big," his mother said. "Ask for more money, and if you don't get it, *then* lower your price."

George added three zeroes to the price and settled in to read a comic book.

A while later, George's mother noticed he was putting the table away. The turtle dish was nowhere in sight.

"Where's the turtle?" she asked.

"I sold it," George said.

His mother's eyes went wide. "You mean you really got $1,000 for it?"

"Kinda," George said, reaching into his pockets. "I traded it for these two $500 frogs."

They Learned Their Lesson

A TEACHER in a one-room schoolhouse urged his students to think before speaking. "Always count to 50 before speaking," he advised. "And if it's something really important, count to 100."

The next day, while standing next to the wood stove, he noticed all the children were watching him closely and moving their lips. After a few minutes, they all said at once, "Ninety-eight, ninety-nine, one hundred, your coat's on fire!"

All in a Day's Work

THE HEAD START teacher asked my 4-year-old grandson, "What does your daddy do?"

"He works at the paper mill," Matthew replied.

"That's a good way to make money," the teacher said.

"No," Matthew said, "he makes toilet paper."

—*Lucille Blazek*
Oconto Falls, Wisconsin

Shame on You, Santa

ON CHRISTMAS, Bobby's grandmother asked, "Did you see Santa Claus last night?"

"No, ma'am, I didn't," Bobby said. "It was too dark. But I heard what he said when he stubbed his toe on the bedpost."

"Now that I've experienced walking in high heels, I'm not so anxious to grow up."

"I planted a rock garden, Dad."

Sorry to Disturb You

THE TELEPHONE rang in the office of a brilliant surgeon. When the doctor answered it, a small voice inquired, "Who is this?"

The doctor immediately recognized the voice of his young son and replied, "The smartest man in the world."

"I beg your pardon," the boy said politely. "I have the wrong number."

Having a Great Time...

A 4-YEAR-OLD attended a prayer meeting with his parents. That night, when he knelt to say his bedtime prayers, he said, "Dear Lord, we had a good time at church tonight. I wish You could have been there."

Heaven someday?"

Johnny replied, "Oh, yes, I want to go *someday*. I was afraid you were fixin' up a load to go *now*."

—Andy Cubit
Oelwein, Iowa

'I'd Like to Propose a Toast'

AS OUR family sat down for Thanksgiving dinner, my husband asked if anyone wanted to give a special toast. Our 4-year-old granddaughter, nicknamed "Pixie", said she had one.

Everyone raised their glasses, and my husband asked, "Okay, Pixie, what's your favorite toast?"

Pixie replied, "Cinnamon!"

—Barbara Junge
Nashville, Illinois

All Things in Good Time

A PREACHER was telling a group of 8-year-olds about the joys of going to Heaven. "Everyone who wants to go to Heaven, stand up," he called out. All the children jumped to their feet except Johnny.

"What's the matter, Johnny?" the preacher asked. "Don't you want to go to

Struggling Musician

MRS. WILSON was an excellent teacher but a very poor musician. One day the teacher who usually played the piano called in sick. Mrs. Wilson hadn't played a note in 30 years and struggled to play a familiar tune with one finger.

After class, little Billy approached her and complimented her performance. "You play much better than our regular teacher," he said. "Miss Shaw has to use both hands."

Going Up, Up, Up

ON HIS first visit to New York City, a small boy got on an elevator at the Empire State Building with his father. The elevator shot up, whizzing past the 50th floor. The child looked up and asked, "Daddy, does God know we're coming?"

Saints Preserve Us!

THE SUNDAY SCHOOL teacher asked her 3- and 4-year-old pupils, "Do you remember who St. Matthew was?" No one answered. "Does anyone remember who St. Mark was?" Still no answer.

"Surely someone remembers who Peter was," the teacher said. The room was silent. Finally a small voice ventured, "I think he was a wabbit." —*Donald Novak Montfort, Wisconsin*

Gone to the Dogs

SIX-YEAR-OLD Craig was always bringing home stray animals. But when he brought home a filthy mongrel dog, his mother put her foot down.

"This dog even has bad breath," his mother said.

Craig shot back indignantly, "He wants to be fed, not kissed!"

Who's Driving Here?

THE CHILDREN were asked to draw their favorite scene from the Bible. One boy gave the teacher a drawing of a sports car, with a bearded man in the front seat and a man and woman in back.

"What Bible story is this picture supposed to illustrate?" the puzzled teacher asked.

The child explained, "That's God driving Adam and Eve out of the Garden of Eden."

Looking for The Exit

LITTLE TOMMY was getting tired of the pastor's sermon. After much squirming, he finally whispered to his mother, "If we give him the money now, will he let us out?"

Prayers and Bears

AT BREAKFAST, Grandma asked 4-year-old Susie if she'd said her prayers the night before.

"Well, I started to," Susie said. "Then I thought God must get so tired of hearing 'Now I lay me down to sleep'. So I told him the story of the three bears instead." —*Elverna Leist LeRoy, Minnesota*

"That grandson of mine—are those long pants or short pants?"

Sticking It Out

A LITTLE BOY told his teacher he had a stomachache. The teacher sent him to see the principal.

Ten minutes later, the child returned. His shoulders were thrown back, and his midsection was stuck out as far as it would go.

"Why are you walking that way?" the teacher asked.

"I told the principal I had a stomachache," the lad replied. "And he said if I could stick it out until noon, he'd take me home."

As He Should

THE TEACHER was getting acquainted with her new class on the first day of kindergarten. "And what does your father do?" she asked one little girl.

"Whatever my mother tells him," the little girl replied.

Easy Question

"CHARLES, can you tell us what a synonym is?" the teacher asked.

"I know that," her pupil answered. "A synonym is a word you use when you can't spell the other one."

She Was All Wet

THE SUNDAY SCHOOL teacher told her young charges, "Now, children, you must never do anything in private that you wouldn't do in public."

"Hurray!" shouted one boy. "No more baths!"

Light Work

"PAPA, what do you do all day long at the office?" the little girl inquired.

Her father, absorbed in reading the newspaper, answered distractedly, "Oh, nothing."

The girl thought for a moment, then asked, "How do you know when you're through?"

"Here comes another one we'll get to bet that we aren't twins."

Teenage Logic

A TEENAGER pointed to the crumpled fender on the family car. "Great news, Dad," he said brightly. "You haven't been pouring those insurance payments down the drain after all."

Portrait Artist

A 5-YEAR-OLD girl was sitting at a table, concentrating on a drawing. Now and then she'd hold it up and examine it carefully, then start working on it again.

"What are you drawing, dear?" her mother asked.

"I am drawing God," she announced.

Her mother was a bit startled. "Why, darling, you can't draw God. No one really knows what He looks like."

"Well," the girl said placidly, "they will when I'm finished."

Is There a Doctor in The House?

A MAN TOLD his wife wearily, "I'm sure all three of our kids are going to be doctors."

"Why is that, dear?"

"Because they never come when we call them."

Leaves Much to Be Desired

WHILE visiting my sister, her young daughter helped me set the table for the evening meal. I soon realized the table wasn't big enough to seat everyone.

"Katie," I asked my niece, "does your mom have any leaves for this table?"

Katie gave me a quizzical glance, then disappeared. A few minutes later, she returned with two handfuls of leaves from the backyard. "Here," she said. "I picked up some leaves for the table."

—Sister Judy Norwick
Kaukauna, Wisconsin

A Snappy Explanation

MY NEPHEW was trying to explain to his mother how he broke her kitchen window. "I was cleaning my slingshot," he said, "and it went off". —J. Hampsch
Los Angeles, California

What's the Hang-Up Here?

WHEN my 4-year-old grandson Travis came to visit, I asked him to be a good little boy and hang up his jacket. He looked at me, bewildered, and said, "But, Grandma, it doesn't hang up. It only hangs down!"

—*Bernice Kozlowski*
Wausau, Wisconsin

Fast-Growing Crop

ONE EVENING, my husband and I were planting our vegetable garden. Our 4-year-old granddaughter watched for a while, but was in bed before we spread mothballs around the garden to keep rabbits away.

The next morning, our granddaughter went out to see the garden. She quickly ran back inside, exclaiming, "Grandma, your marshmallows are coming up already!" —*Blanche Lochman*
Slippery Rock
Pennsylvania

Skip the Sandpaper

MY 3-year-old always spent a long time drying herself after a bath. When I asked Jackie why she needed to dry off so thoroughly, she replied, "So I won't rust."

—*Irene Lynn*
Smithfield, Pennsylvania

This Isn't Made Up

THREE-YEAR-OLD T.J. was intently watching me apply my makeup. As I put mascara on my lashes, he asked, "Grandma, why are you putting that on?"

"I'm making myself beautiful for Grandpa," I told him.

"Well, don't make yourself too beautiful," he warned, "or Grandpa won't recognize you."

—*Delores Rappleye*
Fort Bragg, California

A Tough Nut to Crack

AT CHRISTMAS, our family was sharing a bowl of unshelled peanuts. Our 3-year-old daughter took a peanut from the bowl, handed it to her father, and said, "Daddy, unbutton this for me." —*Mrs. Don Henry*
Goff, Kansas